RESTORING THE
Soul TO EDUCATION

*Equity Closes the
Achievement Gap*

Dr. Carmen I. Ayala · Bea Young · Michael L. Kilgore

Writers of the Round Table Press
PO Box 1603, Deerfield, IL 60015
www.roundtablecompanies.com

Editor: **Duane Barnes**

Round Table Companies
Publisher: **Corey Michael Blake**
President: **Kristin Westberg**
Editor: **Agata Antonow**
Cover Designer: **Sunny DiMartino**
Interior Designer: **Christy Bui**
Proofreaders: **Adam Lawrence, Carly Cohen**

Printed in the United States of America

First Edition: September 2019
10 9 8 7 6 5 4 3 2 1

Library of Congress Cataloging-in-Publication Data
Restoring the soul to education: equity closes the achievement gap /
Carmen I. Ayala, Bea Young, and Michael L. Kilgore.—1st ed. p. cm.
ISBN Paperback: 978-1-61066-077-8
ISBN Digital: 978-1-61066-148-5
Library of Congress Control Number: 2019909606

Writers of the Round Table Press and the logo are trademarks of
Writers of the Round Table, Inc.

We, the coauthors, share in this dedication to Carmen's ever-supportive father.

Dedication to Efrain Ayala

In gratitude and love.
I am who I am because you showed and taught me
    To believe in a higher Power,
    To never give up, and
    To push forward for myself and others.
You are now an angel that continues to guide me from
Heaven. I love you.

Iris

CONTENTS

> 1990: Storm of Nature Changes the Dynamics and Destiny of D202
>
> 2003: The Cultural Storm Creates White Residents' Fear
>
> 2005: District's Awakening Awareness around Difference
>
> A National Awareness: No Child Left Behind
>
> Hiring the Team Comes with Resistance
>
> The Curriculum Strategy
>
> The Cultural Responsiveness Strategy
>
> Measurable Achievement Results
>
> What Made the Difference in Lowering the Achievement Gap?
>
> Postscript: A Moral Compass in the Storms

> Building on Lessons Learned at Plainfield District 202
>
> Another Storm: An Intentional One
>
> Five Major Initiatives Emerge
>
> Beginning with the Cultural Audit Data
>
> Responding to Resistance
>
> Moving Forward with Inclusive Behaviors
>
> Grounding District 98's Change Effort in Cultural Responsiveness
>
> Measuring Achievement Results
>
> Achievement Results at District 98
>
> Two Systemic Processes Close the Gap . . . Again

WHY YOU NEED TO READ THIS BOOK

The gap.

The damned, frustrating, vexing, hindering, contemptible
(choose one) gap between the achievement of White students vs.
students of color.
The gap barely closed in fifty years.
More money, more programs, more plans devised to solve
the problem
> *. . . to no avail.*

But we did it.
Not only did we close the achievement gap, but ALL students—
White, Black, Brown
> *. . . rose together.*

Dynamic collaboration over ten years . . .
> *—an educator/consultant focusing on diversity, cultural*
> *responsiveness, and equity*
> *—a district superintendent who implemented the process*
> *—a board of education president who supported the goals*
> *—an assistant superintendent who carried the ball.*

They proved it could be done.
> *And then it was done again.*

That's what this book is about. It's a step-by-step systemic process
> *. . . not a quick fix.*

It's the result of years of experience by the authors—teaching
experiences, life experiences, and effective application of lessons learned.

—Duane Barnes, Editor

AUTHORS' SOUL JOURNEYS

Each of the authors came to this project by different paths, under different circumstances. This book is about life experiences, passion, and advocacy. Our authors begin by sharing the soul journeys that propelled them to create this book.

Soul Journey: Dr. Carmen I. Ayala

I know the feeling of being an outsider, being the first Latino family to move into an all-White neighborhood . . .
　I know what it's like to be called a "spic" . . .
　I know what it's like to be threatened with a scholarship loss because the college needed to make a "cut" somewhere . . . to two Latinas . . .

What brought me to coauthor this book was a boy named Abel. Abel was a freckled nine-year-old second-grade Latino student who should have been in third grade. He had big, brown expressive eyes and was a talker. Whenever we'd have conversations about a story, he would chime right in and express insightful comments about the story, plot, or the characters. But Abel had one problem. He couldn't read. He couldn't read in Spanish, and he certainly couldn't read in English because he barely understood it. He was already in the special education referral process and was being "tested" to determine if he had a learning disability. Abel was also becoming a bit of a behavior problem.

I started working with Abel and asked his teacher, a Latina herself, if I could take Abel into an earlier first-grade group. Abel fit right in. Before long, he started to pick up the names of the letters and their sounds. He was starting to read some words in Spanish. I kept Abel with the first-grade group and also with the second-grade group. By the end of the first semester, he was absorbing first-grade books like a sponge.

After the end of the first semester, I attended Abel's diagnostic meeting.

His teacher shared that she had walked by his desk and asked him what he was doing. He looked up at her and said, "*Maestra, estoy leyendo.* (Teacher, I'm reading)." Not believing him, she asked him to read to her. To her surprise, Abel beautifully read out loud from his book; she was dumbfounded. The original recommendation for special education was rescinded because Abel did not need special education services. He just needed someone to help him crack the code of a language he couldn't understand. I left that school that year and lost track of Abel, but, even twenty-five years later, I can still see his wide-smiled, freckled-face.

I became a teacher because I love children and because my parents had always talked to us about the value and importance of a good education. I became a bilingual teacher because I grew up in a bilingual home and I saw and experienced firsthand the struggles of people, like Abel, when they cannot speak English. I was also very disturbed by the large dropout rate of Latinos and the small percentages going on to college.

When I left teaching and entered the administrative ranks, I kept working to "crack the code" for all the Abels who might be condemned to paths beneath their potential. I recall sitting in a meeting with fellow high school leaders where I was the only and first Latina administrator, when one of my colleagues casually noted that, "You know, Latino parents don't really value education." An awkward silence followed. My emotions surged. I could no longer contain myself as I expressed my concern over such an unconscious and demeaning remark.

This marked a turning point in that district where events—described in this book—would set me on a path to develop a comprehensive initiative that would result in incredible gains for all students.

I had the good fortune to be a part of these journeys. I invite you to join in.

Carmen I. Ayala

Soul Journey: Bea Young

In 1960, proudly armed with my University of Chicago degree in education, I was excitedly looking forward to my first assignment: teaching social studies in an all-Black high school on Chicago's West Side. As I reviewed the texts for the course I was to teach, I was shocked to find a sentence that read, "Slavery was good for the slaves." Further on, opening a chapter on Africa, the first sentence was "For all Africa gave to the world, it might as well have been on the moon." I was stunned and knew I couldn't use these texts in *any* high school, especially with students whose history and culture were different from mine.

As I got to know my students, I told them their history books had omissions and misinformation and we were going to create a new and true history. Arming them with borrowed tape recorders, I asked them to interview their parents, grandparents, other relatives, and neighbors. Following through, they discovered the missing pages of Black history not found in traditional American history. They poured their hearts and souls into their research, creating a book that would be proudly displayed in 1963 at the Emancipation Proclamation Centennial Celebration at Chicago's McCormick Place.

With this success, my students and I created a skit, "I, Too, Sing America," the title borrowed from Langston Hughes's poem. Using quotes from Black history over the centuries, we were invited to present the skit in high schools throughout Illinois and the Midwest. Remember: this was the early 1960s.

Because of my intense knowledge of and commitment to Black history, I was invited to coauthor a section of the Freedom Schools' Curriculum for the Mississippi Civil Rights Summer of 1964. There, I experienced cross-burnings and frequent jailings, and witnessed the daily abuse of Black parents, standing in line to register to vote for the first time.

In 1965, I was asked to create the first Education Services Department of the Illinois Commission on Human Relations. This gave me the unique opportunity to help school districts across Illinois facilitate the integration of Black and White high school students. We listened to conflicting views and helped students, their communities, and the school administrators reach consensus. These sessions worked, much to the surprise of the Illinois State Police who arrived in tanks and hard hats in case our collaborative method didn't work.

I left the public sector in 1976 and had the opportunity to help dozens of major corporations change their culture through the implementation of a systemic approach to valuing racial and gender diversity. But my soul remained centered on returning to the world of education.

And, finally, these heartening and exciting school district experiences you're about to read brought all my skills to the test and created the foundation for this book. I hope you'll mine it for your students and the world in which they live.

Bea Young

Soul Journey: Michael Kilgore

Coming home to the mountains of Southwest Virginia for spring break from a chastening first year at Brown University, I could finally relax. Solitary hikes in cool mountain air. No discomfort about the hillbilly accent I'd learned to mask from prep school roommates. I was the only one of my high school class of 121 not destined for a life underground in the coal mines.

Then it all changed. My Piedmont flight back to Providence was scheduled for April 5, 1968. On the evening news on April 4, my parents and I watched the grim narrative of Martin Luther King's assassination. Convinced that King was an agent of the Communist Party, my father, whom I worshipped, uttered the words "good riddance." It was the first—and last—violent confrontation I ever had with this compassionate genius, whose moral compass was so focused, he could stop asinine arguments by simply raising an eyebrow.

The ride to the Tri-Cities Airport was silent. The pilot on the flight to Rhode Island made a point of flying low over Washington, DC. We could see dense clouds of smoke as flames engulfed blocks of the city. Arriving at the airport that evening, a coterie of friends decided to spend the evening at one of the sixteen-room cottages overlooking Narragansett Bay rather than heading directly back to school. After a lavish dinner of lobster, talk quickly turned from King's assassination and the ensuing riots in Baltimore, Washington, Chicago—just to name a few—to conversation about yachts, sailing conditions in the bay, and the challenges required for upcoming final exams.

In that moment, I realized I belonged nowhere. I was an outsider in this world of privilege and had the required fake accent. The mountains I loved I could never again call home. The place of my youth was scarred by racial ignorance as ugly as the strip mines that slashed its proud peaks.

Being an outsider marginalizes people. Understanding and changing that dynamic became a driving force in my life. While I was training director at the University of Chicago Hospitals and Clinics, African American colleagues shared countless stories of how they trained their White counterparts, only to be passed over for the promotion. There, I had to tell the grieving partner of the first gay man to die of AIDS in Chicago that he could not have his partner's body for burial.

During the '90s, I worked closely with Bea Young as we partnered to help corporate leaders understand the impact of outsider and insider status in a diverse workforce. We had the joy of working together again when I coauthored both the Plainfield District 202 and Berwyn North District 98 cultural audits. Working now as a member of this writing team continues that journey. It's my hope this small book with a big heart can help point the way to the intersection where the privileged few and the marginalized many find common ground.

Michael Kilgore

Left to right: Bea Young, Dr. Carmen I. Ayala, Michael Kilgore

PREFACE

The Coleman Report Paved the Way

In 1966, a graduate student moved through wet springtime Washington, DC, streets with a sheaf of printouts under his arm. Each page was fresh from the mainframe computers of the Educational Testing Service in Princeton, New Jersey.

The graduate student approached a very modest hotel, walked up the stairs, and knocked. The man who answered the door was Johns Hopkins sociologist James Coleman. Days before, he had checked himself into this hotel with one change of clothing. Each day, someone brought him fresh printouts and analysis. The papers were stacked around the room as he worked.

The work that absorbed Coleman so much—that kept him awake for hours into the nights—was designed to examine how students experienced access to education. Over a decade after May 17, 1954, when, in the case of Brown v. Board of Education, the US Supreme Court found segregation in schools to be unconstitutional, many knew there were still gaps. It was understood that equality had not come to education the way it was meant to, but there was no viable proof. There was no nationwide standardized testing, and no one had compared the school performance of different groups of children. No one had looked at the bigger questions of equal access in education.

Until one man holed himself up in a hotel and waited for his printouts, based on analysis from surveys completed by sixty thousand teachers and six hundred thousand students across four thousand public schools in the United States. In 1966, Coleman would publish his 737-page report, *Equality of Educational Opportunity*, which became known as the Coleman Report.[1] Among other findings, it would document the achievement gap, offering the first concrete evidence that African American children were testing several grade levels behind their White counterparts in reading and mathematics.

---

1 James S. Coleman, et al., *Equality of Educational Opportunity* (Washington, DC: National Center for Educational Statistics, US Government Printing Office, 1966).

The achievement gap between children of color and White children remains largely unresolved nationally since it was first documented in the Coleman Report. Coleman's study was a result of the Civil Rights Act of 1964, Section 402, which required the commissioner of education to conduct a survey with a report to President Johnson and Congress "concerning the lack of availability of equal educational opportunities for individuals by reason of race, color, religion, or national origin in public educational institutions."[2]

The fiftieth anniversary of the Coleman Report occurred in 2016, but educational equality remains a goal rather than a reality for many of our nation's students. As late as 2019, news reports were documenting that school audits at public schools were still revealing startling achievement gaps.

The story you are about to read is about two Illinois school districts which did succeed in closing that gap in 2010 and 2017 by addressing educational equity for all children of color. You will read about the challenges these school districts faced and the systemic approach they used on their journey to educational equity.

> **The achievement gap between children of color and White children remains largely unresolved nationally since it was first documented in the Coleman Report.**

Educational equity is a set of practices developed by a school district to ensure educational outcomes are not negatively impacted by race, ethnicity, dominant language, family income, or gender, among others. It posits that all children must be taught to the same standards—that's the "equal" part. And, importantly, it provides organizational cultural responsiveness to effect positive outcomes for all—that's the "equitable" part of the equation.

---

2   Coleman, et al., *Equality of Educational Opportunity*, iii.

Equality vs Equity in Education

Equality = SAMENESS	Equity = FAIRNESS
Equality is about **sameness**. It promotes fairness and justice by giving everyone the same thing.	Equity is about **fairness**. It's about making sure that each student gets access to the opportunities they need.
But it can only work if everyone starts from the **same** place. In this example equality only works if everyone is the same height, ability, race, and gender.	Sometimes our differences and/or history can create barriers to participation. So, we must **first** ensure **equity** before we can enjoy equality.

Restoring the Soul to Education: Equity Closes the Achievement Gap narrates the success stories of Plainfield District 202, a large diverse district in the southwestern suburbs of Chicago, and Berwyn North District 98, a largely Hispanic elementary district just outside the city's boundary. The book gives the specifics of what worked (and what didn't) in closing the gap in these two districts; the elements of how to navigate the change process through inevitable storms and some of the shoals to expect on the educational equity journey. Additionally, there are tools provided for those who wish to take this journey.

PART I
What We Did

1 THE PLAINFIELD DISTRICT 202 SUCCESS STORY

A Journey through the Storms of Nature and Culture

1990: Storm of Nature Changes the Dynamics and Destiny of D202

On August 28, 1990, Dr. John Harper first noticed something odd while he was talking to his physical education teacher in the school's gymnasium. Above the teacher's head, John could see objects whirling in the sky, spinning higher and higher. They paused in their conversation, realizing the severe weather—which enveloped the Plainfield, Illinois, area that day—was about to do a great deal more than just "storming."

As a professional in his first principalship, John had spent the entire summer getting ready for the start of school. Now, on the last day of teacher orientation and one day before students filled the halls, his knowledge of the school allowed him to act quickly, and both he and the teacher headed to the center of the building. There had been no warnings on the radio, but it was clear they were in danger.

Hurrying down a hallway lined with glass windows, they reached a door that refused to budge. Though it was unlocked, the pressure in the building had built to such a degree that the door was sealed. A ceiling tile hit the floor beside them and broke into pieces, as lights fell nearby and shattered.

Both men had taught their students how to ride out a tornado, so they knew what to do: they tucked themselves in against the wall of the hallway, covered their heads, and prayed.

When the wind slowed down and the cacophony of noise subsided, they picked their way slowly through the transformed school, stepping carefully over broken tile, exposed wires, and metal brackets, as the smell of smoke filled their noses.

The school had stood since the 1970s and had not been designed to withstand tornadoes. Most of the fifteen teachers and staff still inside the school had found shelter in the bathrooms built of cinder block. Moving room by room throughout the building, John discovered that more than half the building had been destroyed, but thankfully everyone was safe.

The clocks left on the walls had all stopped at 3:36 p.m., meaning most of the staff would have headed home by then. He hoped they were safe as he reviewed the wreckage throughout the school.

When John finally emerged into the outside world and stepped into the hot late-summer day, it took him a moment to get his bearings. From where he was now standing, he had never been able to see the Louis Joliet Mall on Mall Loop Drive. Now, he realized the subdivision that separated the school and the mall was gone! Nothing but torn-up earth and pieces of building materials remained. He looked east, and, from his vantage point, saw his own house standing and felt a moment of comfort in knowing his young children and wife were safe.

Suddenly, the air, which had gone still, filled with a loud whir. Looking up, John saw medical helicopters landing, men in uniform jumping onto what had once been the playground area.

John moved down the school hallways with the emergency response team as they called out which usable classrooms would be commandeered for Plainfield's rescue-and-response operation: "This will be the waiting area. We'll use this as our operating room."

On the evening news, millions of Americans learned about the monster F5 tornado that hit Plainfield, Illinois, that day. Cameras invited the country into the nineteen-mile path of destruction caused by the 200 mph winds that killed 29 people and injured 353. Thousands of volunteers from across the state were already heading to Plainfield to pitch in with cleanup and relief.

During the cleanup, the *Chicago Tribune* publicized that, although there was much devastation, Plainfield was a great place to buy a home inexpensively: land was cheap, property taxes were low, and neighbors were helping each other. Located just thirty-five miles southwest of Chicago, it was an easy commute on the Interstate 55 corridor nearby. The papers especially highlighted the Plainfield district's schools as an excellent place to educate children.

One resident was quoted as saying, "After the tornado went through, it's like everyone said, 'Let's move to Plainfield.'" Many Hispanic and

African American Chicagoans had never heard of this possible slice of the American dream until the tornado publicity. They flocked to this village of plain and simple fields.

In 1990, the sixty-four-square-mile school district serving the village and the surrounding rural area consisted of five buildings with thirty-three hundred students. The school population was approximately 96 percent White, 3 percent Hispanic, and 1 percent Asian American.

Twelve years later in 2002, Plainfield School District 202 exceeded eighteen thousand students. New school buildings were being built at the rate of at least one per year. Some years saw three. It was all the district could do just to offer each child a seat.

2003: The Cultural Storm Creates White Residents' Fear

Rapid growth brought revitalization, but also concern. Many long-term White residents were fearful that the presence of Hispanic and African American families and children would diminish the quality of the schools. Thus, when Dr. John Harper took on the role of District Superintendent, twelve years after the tornado hit, other storms were brewing. As he noted, "We were not only getting bigger, but our school demographics were changing. This led to an ensuing struggle between the preservation of a comfortable, traditional lifestyle, and the acceptance of a less familiar, more contemporary way of life.

The resistance was not just the usual "if it ain't broke, why fix it?" mentality seen in many small towns. The demographic changes were demanding people take a look at their assumptions. John had grown up and been educated at a diverse Catholic school, and was comfortable with people of many backgrounds. He began as a Plainfield teacher in 1981, then took on the role of principal right before the tornado. During his tenure over those two decades, he

The demographic changes were demanding people take a look at their assumptions.

didn't remember seeing any explicit racism. In fact, within the predominantly White community, race rarely entered into the discussion at all.

What many people didn't realize was that Plainfield had a hidden and challenging relationship with the Ku Klux Klan. The town had been Illinois' principal center for the KKK starting in the 1920s. It's hard to imagine real estate agents featuring that fact on the brochures they were handing out to Hispanics, African Americans, and other people of color as they made the move to Plainfield in the 1990s. Rapid changes in the school district's population were uncovering deep pain and trauma linked to the area's past.

At the same time, other storms were brewing. John had helped to resolve a bitter teachers' strike in 2001, and those wounds lingered in many teachers' minds. His becoming superintendent in 2002 also meant a change in leadership just as the district was examining some of these challenges.

The physical growth of the district through 2002 was creating its own kind of storm. There were hundreds of new teachers hired and twenty-four hundred new students each year. As more and more schools were built around the district, children had to be moved from school to school, relative to the proximity of the schools and where they lived. Many parents became upset when their children had to leave their familiar setting for something unknown. With no coordinated curriculum in place, some students found themselves unprepared when they opened their textbooks in a classroom at their new school, while others found themselves bored, having already learned what was being taught.

Thus, the 1990 tornado of nature set a series of metaphorical tornadoes in motion. By 2002, the sensation of spinning could be felt throughout the district. Plainfield was in the midst of an institutional anxiety attack.

2005: District's Awakening Awareness around Difference

Ryan Jackson's parents didn't have an appointment when they came to see John soon after he had stepped into the superintendent role. When he saw how upset they were, he sat them down in his office and listened. It was an emotional meeting as the couple told him about how much their youngest son, Ryan, had wanted to join the basketball team at Ira Jones Middle School. He had been cut from the team, and his parents knew it wasn't because he lacked talent. They were convinced it was an issue of racial discrimination.

The Jacksons had spoken to the coach, the athletic director, and the school's principal before finally visiting John that day. As he listened, the Jacksons described their son's long list of achievements and the ways he had contributed to teams on which he'd played.

John made some calls in search of answers and offered comfort to the family. He spoke with the principal and shared what he'd heard from the Jacksons. The school's principal investigated the situation quickly. He heard that Ryan had been seen in the hallways being disruptive, and that a judgment call had been made prior to tryouts. Ryan was invited back onto the team and played until the end of that year, when he and his family moved away from District 202.

This early experience with the Jacksons helped to make John aware of the differences within the district he would be facing as it became more diverse. As a result, he found himself looking at his schools through a different lens and with different questions: Which students took part in the Advanced Placement courses? Which were in Special Education? Which were being disciplined? What about the social environment? Who was involved in extracurricular activities? Research showed that children who were engaged in sports and extracurricular activities were higher achievers. So, John decided to look at participation.

At a school football game, he realized, "The team itself was fairly diverse with a mixture of White, Black, and Hispanic kids. But then at half-time, the band came on the field. They sounded great, but all were White children. As I looked at the cheerleaders on the sidelines, I realized they all were White."

John investigated further. "Tennis was all White. Basketball was all White. Music was all White. We had a young woman who had won a national version of The Voice in her home country in South America, but who wouldn't even try out for musicals or chorus. The more I walked about, the more I realized the same pattern existed throughout all of our schools. Parents of color were not involved, and their talented children were not participating."

> . . . he found himself looking at his schools through a different lens and with different questions.

His observations led John to question why that was. He began to realize it was not just personal choice or preference. From his own childhood, he remembered signing up for clubs because he knew his friends were going to be in the same groups. The district had to become more welcoming for students interested in joining after-school activities. As things stood, the issue was self-perpetuating: since the district did little to encourage diversity in clubs, students were not joining clubs where they felt they might not belong. In addition, subtle racist accusations were made about the students' abilities.

At the other extreme, John discovered there were a disproportionate number of Black and Hispanic boys in the so-called Freshman Academy, a "school-within-a-school" designed to handle "at-risk" students. The Black and Hispanic population had grown to 20 percent. In contrast, 40 percent of the disciplinary actions involved students of color. John remembered the initial reaction of one high school administrator: "These kids just haven't yet had time to acclimate to our higher expectations." Hearing that comment, John knew that the district was experiencing a cultural divide.

Seeing the problem was the first step, and eager to share what he saw, John opened up a conversation among his leadership. With a focus on the increasingly diversified student population, he questioned how the district was engaging this new student population formally through the curriculum and informally through sports and extracurricular activities. He knew they needed to expand access to both, but nobody had an answer as to how.

Lacking clarity, John still had an important decision to make. "We could have allowed ourselves to focus our attention exclusively upon student growth and school construction," he explained. "I insisted, however, that we shift our focus to the learning taking place in our schools."

A National Awareness: No Child Left Behind

At the time John was reevaluating how the district helped students achieve, the national context for education was changing. At the July 2000 annual convention of the NAACP, President George W. Bush famously announced his intent to address the "soft bigotry of low expectations" in education, and set the stage for our story with the No Child Left Behind

Act of 2001 (NCLB). Passed with broad bipartisan support and signed into law January 8, 2002, NCLB required all public schools receiving federal funding to administer statewide standardized tests annually to all students.

Most importantly, the law also required test results to be separated by nine different groupings: White, Black, Hispanic, Asian/Pacific Islander, Native American, multiracial, low income, limited English language proficiency, and students with disabilities (special education). Collecting this data was mandated as an effort to show how well schools were serving all children. Prior to NCLB, test results were simply averaged out. It was now important to monitor and support students that fell into these nine groups, especially if there were achievement gaps between the groups. The results of each school district became public information.

Seeing the problem was the first step . . .

Any school that had one of these nine groups not meeting a predetermined target was deemed as "failing" or not performing. Results of the standardized tests were compared on a school/district basis within each state. If a school's results were repeatedly poor, then steps were taken to improve it. While the intent was to identify problem areas and share best practices, the scores became de facto competitions among schools and districts. There was, therefore, pressure to keep scores high and to encourage all students to succeed in accordance with the tests.

While NCLB has been a controversial program overall, No Child Left Behind forced District 202 to start understanding the differing demographics of the students they served and how well the district was doing the job of educating them. The metrics required by NCLB flooded their problems with light. The standardized testing across the state allowed Plainfield to see which areas needed work and where they were doing well.

Hiring the Team Comes with Resistance

Because of Plainfield's shifting demographics and its meteoric growth, John knew he needed to create a coordinated curriculum to serve all students and a new learning culture. This was done within the context of a predominantly conservative all-White board of education. These two priorities became the guideposts for John's direction. Thankfully, he had the support of Mike Kelly, the president of the board of education at that time and a long-time resident of Plainfield. Kelly, elected for several terms, knew that board members often came to the table to "fix" things that had nothing to do with the success of the students. He supported John by advising board members to keep their focus on what was good for all of the kids.

John's first major change initiative was the hiring of Dr. Carmen I. Ayala into the new role of Assistant Superintendent for Curriculum and Instruction in 2005. Dr. Ayala held a PhD in educational leadership and policy studies plus an MBA in administration. She came with twenty-two years of experience at all levels of education and with expertise in the area of ELs (English learners). As a Latina, Carmen knew firsthand how children of color were marginalized, usually unintentionally, by educators. She became the first educator of color on the leadership team at the district level.

The year Carmen was hired, fewer than 3 percent of the teachers and administrators were of color, while the students of color represented 20 percent of the school population. John had to start bringing additional teachers and administrators of color on board to address the growing concerns of the African American and Hispanic communities who felt their children were being marginalized. Having Spanish-speaking teachers on the faculty would also help Hispanic parents feel more comfortable asking questions if they didn't speak English. "We knew our leadership had to progress toward looking like our students," said John. "So, we put dollars into recruiting and hiring people of color. We wanted a staff that reflected the changing makeup of the community. And we knew we could not compromise quality."

> We were at a crossroads to do the right thing. We had to serve all children from the district.

John made some excellent choices when it came to early hires; however, he made one choice that complicated the entire transformational effort. Intending to diversify the district, he hired an African American principal to head up one of the elementary schools. Unfortunately, his performance was subpar, and, within only a few months, John realized he had made a substantial error. Looking back and doing some investigating to determine how his poor performance came to be, John learned that this principal's previous employer had expunged damaging information from his file. Ultimately, John recommended to the board of education that the principal be released.

"This was difficult for me," Carmen remembered. As his evaluator, she felt great empathy for someone else she imagined might feel like an outsider. She was also eager to see more leadership of color, knowing it would help the district thrive. "I tried to internally reconcile issues of fairness with issues of performance. After a few months, it was clear that the district could not have provided more support. He simply did not have the skills needed to lead a school."

This most sensitive issue resulted in a meeting with Operation PUSH, the civil rights group. Present were Board President Mike Kelly, Dr. Harper, Jesse Jackson Sr., and the principal with his two attorneys. The question was whether PUSH should intervene. Mike Kelly remembers the challenge of that meeting and its outcome: "We repeatedly stated that we knew we needed a more diverse staff. PUSH decided not to pursue the case. But Plainfield's African American community was understandably upset with the decision, as this individual was the first Black person hired into the district's administration."

Having to release the first Black principal highlighted the delicate nature of decisions being made. Mike Kelly, thinking back on the often-turbulent meetings of the board of education, recalled: "We were at a crossroads to do the right thing. We had to serve all children from the district. Some White community members wanted to blame 'them' for being here; but it wasn't their fault. They were just here."

Conversations around lack of engagement, disproportionate disciplinary actions for students of color, assumptions about fitting in, and marginalizing students based upon racial stereotypes were not easy. "When we were together—once a month—the conversations about diversity became emotional. Often people left crying," grieved John. "We were not yet equipped to have these conversations."

The White community's desire to protect their children was natural but also an unconscious form of racism. Assumptions about students of color were being put forth, including a belief that "these kids are coming into the district and pulling down the scores of our (White) kids." Such accusations were not only being made by students and parents—they were also being expressed by some members of the staff and the board.

Other acts of racism weren't subtle at all. It was subsequently learned through the district's cultural audit that some parents who only spoke Spanish were being told by support staff, "Come back when you can speak English." At another point, the district hired a Black director of assessment and accountability, a professional whose skills in data analysis were sought by the Illinois State Board of Education. Some administrators at District 202 made comments about her diction, voice, and presentation—things that had nothing to do with her knowledge or performance but were used in pointing out how she was "different" or "less than."

Infighting was also present. John found himself needing to play an uncomfortable role supporting Carmen when he discovered a small faction that was reacting negatively to her having been hired. He intercepted program decisions that were being made without Carmen's awareness, decisions that were causing confusion and undermining her position.

Additionally, some faculty were resisting John's visionary initiatives, which Carmen had been charged to put in place. District 202 teacher, principal, and district administrator Joan Woolwine said, "[Some] teachers initially hated these changes. From initially reluctant teachers to skeptical members of the board of education, the district's impending transformation was made more challenging by the racial mistrust within the community and schools, which easily could have choked any reform, regardless of its efficacy."

The intensity of emotion coming from the community highlighted the district's need for professional support to navigate these challenges and help people with differing backgrounds to hear one another. It was clear more was at stake than one school or even one district. The problem echoed a much larger conversation the country was having. Plainfield was quickly becoming a diverse microcosm of the entire country, with all the fears and assumptions we continue to see today.

The Curriculum Strategy

One of the early partners Carmen wanted to work with was Rhonda Renfro, president of the Curriculum Leadership Institute (CLI). Carmen had to convince the board of education to agree to hire Rhonda. Because of previous work together, Carmen knew CLI could help her create a "learning culture" at the district to address some of the cultural shifts occurring. Carmen had seen how the CLI model got results.

CLI's Model for School Improvement engages stakeholders. It's a "nuts and bolts" systemic approach to building a consistent district-wide curriculum, which aligns both vertically through the grade levels and horizontally across all the buildings within a district:

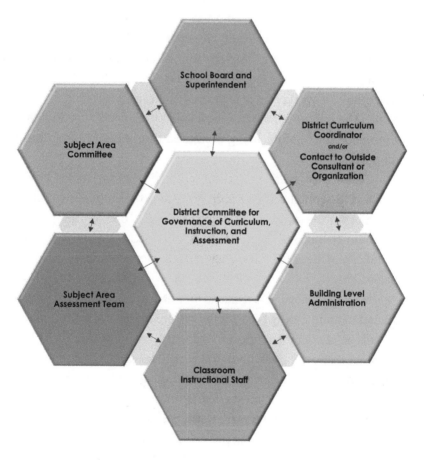

The process was straightforward. There were two major organizational components required: subject area committees (SAC) and a Curriculum Coordinating Council (CCC). An important sidebar is that CLI would not take any district as a client unless it committed to four years. Real change took time.

The SAC was the bottom-up process, which allowed the district's subject area experts to come together to write an instructional plan for each subject area appropriate to each grade level. An important benefit of this process was that teachers throughout a district "owned" the curriculum; it didn't come from "outside." State standards were simply the foundation for the curriculum, but they were not "the" curriculum.

The CCC was a balanced representative group from the district in which members brought their expertise to the table but left their titles at the door. At District 202, the twenty-five-member CCC included members of the board of education, district administrators, principals, assistant principals, parents, and some SAC members. Carmen served as its chair.

Essentially, it worked as a district-wide steering committee, which compiled the instructional plans developed by the SACs, making final recommendations before being presented to the board of education for approval.

The CCC approach encouraged the entire district to become a "learning culture." Essentially, the curriculum became the embodiment of best teaching practices—not just "teaching to the test," one of most frequent criticisms of NCLB. SAC members frequently became mentors for both new and experienced teachers. They came to view themselves as instructional leaders.

As Rhonda described it, "We like to look at the CCC as a representation dedicated to maintaining the systemic nature of the curriculum process. From this perspective, attention to student learning becomes the most important function of the school. Today, with most accreditation models across the nation emphasizing systems thinking, the systemic approach is considered by many the most effective means of accomplishing this."

Rhonda recalled that the early resistance stemmed from three main triggers: "For some, it was fear of the unknown. Some felt coerced. Others simply knew this was going to be really hard work. Two teachers were unwilling to comply with the curriculum changes. They were highly regarded and decided not to use the newly aligned curriculum. They felt entitled to teach the way they always had."

Board President Mike Kelly recalled how important it was that the board of education approve the curriculum. Core to CLI's governance principle was that of participation and informed consent, leading to a culture of accountability. Kelly also understood how difficult it was for board of education members to appreciate why the curriculum initiative was more than just complying with federal regulations. "Because of NCLB, how the state evaluated schools was changing. It was difficult for those on the CCC and board of education to understand. Changing District 202's curriculum was a human enterprise impacting the individual lives of almost thirty thousand children. Simply put, it mattered."

It mattered that all children were being supported, and that meant more accountability when it came to teaching a common curriculum. The administration, principals, teachers, students, and community had to pull together to build a new, diverse, and united District 202 that was also poised to excel academically.

The Cultural Responsiveness Strategy

During this transition phase, a new Illinois Education Association (IEA Union) representative was assigned to District 202. This union representative, like John, was waking up to the reality that some teachers in the district were not intuitively meeting the needs of children of color. She shared her observations with John and recommended the district work with Bea Young as the consultant to guide their cultural change efforts. Bea, at that time, was the founder and president of the Kaleidoscope Group and had navigated diversity storms for over forty years in both corporate and educational institutions. She had been a pioneer in incorporating African American history into traditional history and helped to integrate Black and White students in high schools throughout numerous Illinois school districts in the mid-1960s and '70s.

In the fall of 2005, at the same time the CLI model was being introduced to the district, the Bea Young Associates (BYA) "educational equity journey" was also being introduced to help create the cultural support needed for the educational journey:

Educational Equity Journey

Cultural Audit
Internal: School Districts and Universities
External: Parents and Community

Audit
Report
Anonymous
Feedback

Measurement
and
Accountability

Leadership
Commitment
to
Educational
Equity

Integrate
Learning
with
Systems

Implementation
Systems and
Initiatives

Cultural
Responsiveness
Education

Dr. Harper wanted to introduce this new approach with a powerful impact for all his staff. Bea's team quickly arranged four Diversity and Inclusion Teacher Institute workshop sessions in one day, in two high school auditoriums, training all twenty-four hundred staff, both professional and support. Bea's team moved through the audiences to keep everyone engaged, and the groups were split into sessions of six hundred participants to keep them manageable. Bea recalled that "Our goal was to clarify the intent and meaning of diversity and inclusion using interactive exercises."

Just as the first step of the SAC was a coming together of stakeholders, the first step on the BYA "educational equity journey" was a cultural audit, which involved anonymous interviews and focus groups, conducted both internally and externally, to help identify major hopes and concerns and to give everyone a voice.

BYA interviewed all the board members and the cabinet, and conducted racially and ethnically homogeneous focus groups with representatives at every level of the district, both professional and support staff as well as students. For the external audit, they conducted interviews with community leaders and racial and ethnic focus groups with parents. All of the responses remained anonymous.

After each cultural audit, the superintendent and the board of education, as always, were the first to receive, from the consulting team, a summary of the cultural audit reports. Then all senior leaders, numbering nearly one hundred per session, led by Bea Young, met in feedback sessions to examine key themes. For each theme examined, the anonymous focus group quotes were read aloud by the superintendent and his direct reports. Following is a sample of some quotes from the 2007 cultural audit at District 202:

- *"Teachers and administrators lack understanding of valuing differences and its impact on our success."* (student focus groups)
- *"There is a huge disconnect between the cultural differences of the student population and the board, administrators, and teachers."* (leadership interviews)
- *"We lack a relevant knowledge base related to diversity and equity."* (administrators, teachers, support staff focus groups)
- *"Diverse cultural events appear to be systematically devalued."* (parent focus groups)
- *"New demographics are seen as counter to the district's history."* (community focus groups)

As Bea recalled, "Hearing the anonymous statements from their stakeholders captured the attention of the administrators, principals, and assistant principals whose attendance was required for these feedback sessions."

"This focus group information was very hard for us to hear," shared John. "But the process began with awareness. The anonymous quotes from our stakeholders were dramatic."

As a result of these leadership sessions in 2006–2007, the board of education approved funds for cultural responsiveness training for the over one hundred senior leaders. However, John knew the next steps on the equity journey had to include more than training and professional development. It needed to be systemic, and the process could begin when the issues, uncovered in the cultural audit, were integrated into each part of the five-year strategic plan. Many of the issues and recommendations reflected racial and cultural misunderstandings, lack of communication, and unconscious bias. Thus, incorporating follow-up actions within each of the major district departments would be required to create much-needed accountability and, ultimately, measurement. The equity journey had to connect at all levels and be supported by the superintendent and board of education, with every leader held accountable for cultural responsiveness in their performance reviews.

According to John, five-year plans are one of the key ways to integrate the curriculum and cultural themes and to make all issues actionable while also keeping everyone accountable. "The strategic plan was the key," he said. "We created two five-year plans while I was superintendent. With twenty-nine thousand children, we had grown to be the fourth largest district in Illinois. Given the size of the schools, we knew we had to create continuity. Yet standards had to be the same throughout the district since we were being measured against state standards as well as against other districts in the state."

> He understood that diversity was not a stand-alone initiative . . .

Bea remembered walking into the district conference room one day to see John at the whiteboard. He was capturing what it would take to integrate the results of the cultural audits into all aspects of the five-year strategic plan. According to Bea, "that was when I believed the effort would be successful. He understood that diversity was not a stand-alone initiative but part of a systemic effort." And it did make a difference.

When it came to curriculum matters and cultural shifts, the path forward was not linear and neither was the resistance, which continued well into Carmen's tenure. During her fifth year with the district, the school board determined they would conduct an annual evaluation of Carmen's performance. Since a school board only evaluated the superintendent, it was exceedingly unusual that Carmen's work was up for evaluation.

Differing from tradition, John was not allowed to conduct the evaluation, even though he was her immediate supervisor. Instead, the board hired a consultant who interviewed administrators during the evaluation. The administrators interviewed happened to be those who did not support the changes in the curriculum area.

Carmen hired her own legal counsel and faced the school board. With her counsel sitting next to her, she refuted the negative comments written in the evaluation, line by line, with evidence. After that, the board never confronted her again. Yet, the memory of the long sessions reviewing comment after comment remains with her still: "To this day, that experience was the most difficult and painful of my entire career."

There were other challenges, too, especially once the 2008 recession impacted the district. According to Joan Woolwine, using both the CLI and the BYA models worked very well, though both were impacted by budget cuts. "At the administrator level, we got fabulous training from Bea and her group; but the principals didn't get the train-the-trainer approach to bring it to the teacher level. The diversity training piece was huge when it was first introduced, but we gave teachers only an overview due to recession cutbacks."

During the years that were defined by the recession, planned training for teachers did not move forward other than through annual new staff orientation sessions conducted by BYA. However, Bea introduced to the district her senior associate and expert in cultural responsiveness curriculum, Susan O'Halloran. Sue conducted several subject-specific workshops in collaboration with Carmen to help SAC members infuse cultural responsiveness into the curriculum. (Chapter 6 includes examples of questions and techniques developed by O'Halloran to create culturally responsive curriculum.)

Measurable Achievement Results

As a reminder, at the time of the tornado in 1990, school enrollment was thirty-three hundred and 96 percent White. When the new strategy was implemented at District 202 in 2005, enrollment had grown to eighteen thousand students of which only 80 percent were White. By the time our story ends in 2012, the district counted nearly thirty thousand young people under its charge: 59 percent were White (approximately eighteen thousand) with nearly twelve thousand students of color. These included: 23 percent Hispanic, 9 percent Black, 5 percent Asian/Pacific Islanders, and 4 percent other. Low-income students were about 17 percent and "limited English proficient" about 7 percent, with sixty-nine native languages spoken in the district. The changes were dramatic:[3]

1990	2012
3,300 students	30,000 students
96% White	59% White
0% Black	9% Black
3% Hispanic	23% Hispanic
1% Asian	5% Asian
0% other	4% other
3 buildings, 1 high school	30 buildings, 4 high schools

Before leaving District 202, Carmen provided the board of education with updated student achievement data. Comparison data had been collected starting in 2003–2004, two years prior to the implementation of the curriculum development process and the educational equity journey. Data was compared to four other unit districts of comparable size in the area. A unit district serves children from kindergarten through the twelfth grade. The common data used reflected the performance of students on the Illinois Standards Achievement Test (ISAT) taken from the Illinois district report cards.

Prior to implementing the new curriculum, in 2003–04, 63 percent of all Plainfield students met or exceeded standards in grades three to eight. By 2008–09, three years into the new curriculum, and despite the explosive student enrollment growth, demographic shifts, and budget cost containment, that number had increased to 82 percent. Hispanic students rose from exceeding standards at a rate of 51 percent to 72 percent over the same time period. The same gap closure is also evident for African American students who rose from 43 percent to 75 percent and who met or exceeded the standards (just 7 percent points behind the entire population). In both reading and math, Plainfield District 202's performance

---

3   Illinois School Report Card Data, https://www.isbe.net/pages/illinois-state-report-card-data.aspx.

grew faster than surrounding districts, including growth that was triple the amount of an affluent district nearby.

When students of color were accused of dragging down scores in the district, Carmen responded with data. Consultant Dr. David Thurn was hired to assemble and compare achievement data for children that had spent their entire education in District 202 and data about children that had transferred in. The data showed that the "new" students had better performance and were actually raising district scores.

At one point a board member stated, "All of the diversity initiatives were done at the expense of our White students." However, as students of color were improving their scores, White students were also improving dramatically. Between 2004 and 2009, White students reading performance increased by 16.7 percent and their math performance increased by 17.8 percent, yet another demonstration that taking the equity journey creates higher achievement for all students.

In regard to the two teachers who refused to teach the new curriculum, when the test scores were reviewed for their classrooms, it was discovered that those two classrooms were pulling down the average of the whole school. The lesson was an effective one: regardless of how good a teacher is, everyone adheres to the new curriculum.

Despite some of the painful experiences, the numbers confirmed the value of the effort. "In 2004, District 202 was the lowest performing of the districts in the area," shared Carmen. "By 2010, the district was either the highest performing, or had made the most gains of our neighbors, addressing the achievement gap."

What Made the Difference in Lowering the Achievement Gap?

The important thing to recognize about the concurrent work of CLI and BYA is that both utilize systemic change models, which are in many ways parallel. The District 202 success story relates how the two educational processes—curriculum reform and cultural responsiveness—were intertwined. While rarely in the same rooms together, the work of the two firms shared one common denominator, Carmen Ayala, who because of her position could coordinate their efforts. She made the connection of how the work BYA had undertaken could inform the detailed work of the SACs using CLI's principles.

Both firms had the attentive ear of Dr. John Harper. They also had one important similarity: both were headed by experienced educators who knew the achievement gap could be closed if standards were kept high for all children. And both knew that the ability to measure results could persuade even the nonbelievers.

... the ability to measure results could persuade even the nonbelievers.

Thinking about what was accomplished, Bea remarked, "What worked at Plainfield District 202 was having the right people with the right skill sets. Especially important is the ability to measure change with the achievement gap metrics, which are available to the public. Thus, the final step of the educational equity journey was fulfilled and can continue to be measured."

Many of the issues at Plainfield District 202 were clearly about race, ethnicity, and language, and the story needed to be told to the community. Tom Hernandez, director of community relations since 2006, was handling the district's internal communications and external public relations. Tom was White by birth and his adoptive father was Hispanic and the first Hispanic deputy in the Will County Sheriff's Department. After seeing the data points, Tom saw an opportunity to spread the word about the extraordinary gains at Plainfield District 202, especially in regard to English language learners. The Illinois School Board Journal included an article entitled "The Magnificent Story of District 202" in the journal's January/February 2010 issue.[4]

The data required of NCLB showed that not only was the achievement gap closing within the district, but District 202 was also outperforming both its neighboring wealthier districts as well as exceeding Illinois state standards for all groups in math and reading over a six-year period. By 2011–12, when our portion of the story ends, the results continued to improve despite the effects of the 2008 recession and its impact on school funding and resources.

---

4   Linda Dawson, "The Magnificent Story of District 202: A True Tale of Growing Bilingual Education," *The Illinois School Board Journal* 78, no. 1 (January/February 2010), pp. 14–19.

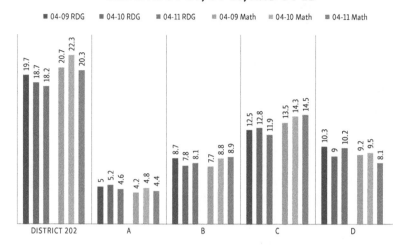

COMPARISON DISTRICTS GROWTH 04-09, 04-10, AND 04-11

■ 04-09 RDG ■ 04-10 RDG ■ 04-11 RDG ■ 04-09 Math ■ 04-10 Math ■ 04-11 Math

The process took years and involved both hard work and challenges. According to John, "The biggest effort and the hardest work was done by the teachers and the kids. They are the ones who closed the gap. This kind of change requires a long-term focus with a sustained effort."

Board of Education President Mike Kelly remembers: "We were moving from being a failing school system to closing the gap for all children in the district. In doing so, we were, in some cases, even exceeding the success of our neighboring districts, which had more resources."

Superintendent John Harper recognized not only the numbers but also the power of how the district's culture was changing. "I began to see the huge resistance from the teachers slowly turn from negativity to acceptance to embracing the process. They became a learning community. Seeing them begin to feel empowered let me know it was worth the effort."

This progress continued into 2018 and demonstrates the sustainability of this systemic approach combining curriculum reform and cultural responsiveness.[5]

5   *2018 Illinois State Report Card* (Springfield, IL: Illinois State Board of Education, 2018), https://www.isbe.net/Documents/2018-State-Report.pdf.

ILLINOIS SCHOOL REPORT CARD 2018 ACHIEVEMENT GAP DATA

	BLACK/WHITE		HISPANIC/WHITE		HISPANIC/BLACK	
	English Language Arts	Math	English Language Arts	Math	English Language Arts	Math
District 202	**15**	**22**	**13**	**18**	2	4
District A	40	41	25	25	15	16
District B	26	34	20	24	6	10
District C	20	25	20	24	**1**	**2**
District D	21	24	20	19	**1**	6

Through the leadership of John Harper, Mike Kelly, and Carmen Ayala, many of the major issues identified in the cultural assessment were addressed successfully. Advanced Placement courses became a process of open enrollment rather than privilege. The Freshman Academy, which singled out Black and Hispanic students, was disbanded. Disciplinary proceedings were removed from the exclusive oversight of the board of education and moved to counselors at the local level who knew the students and their families. Rates of discipline for students of color began to come into line with their enrollment numbers. Most importantly, the district began to celebrate the academic achievement accomplishments of all its students.

Postscript: A Moral Compass in the Storms

John Harper retired from District 202 in 2014. He is now principal of the prestigious college preparatory school Providence Catholic High School in New Lenox, Illinois. During the writing of this book, he shared the following story with Carmen and Bea via email:

My assistant principal stepped into my office this afternoon to let me know I had two visitors in the lobby. They asked her not to share their names. You can probably imagine what was running through my mind!

As soon as I turned the corner into the lobby, I immediately recognized and greeted them, "Mr. and Mrs. Jackson . . ."

Their son Ryan went on to attend Lewis University, and, when he left, he was among the top five scorers in the university's history. He's now playing professional basketball in France, and his agent says he'll get an NBA tryout in two years. The other young man who was also cut from the middle school team is playing professionally in Italy.

I thanked the Jacksons for finding me . . . driving to New Lenox . . . and giving me a gift I'll cherish forever. Specifically, I thanked them for attributing a small part of Ryan's success to a decision I made many years ago. Graciously, they told me they attributed more than a small part of their son's success to me.

2   BERWYN NORTH DISTRICT 98

The Second Success Story—By Choice, Not Chance

As a daughter in the first Latino family to move into an all-White neighborhood, Carmen Ayala understood what it was to be an outsider. Growing up, her father delivered bread to stores regardless of the wind-chill factor, the beating of the rain, or the searing sun. "Pop," as she calls him, worked days. Mom worked the second shift and was home at about 12:30 a.m. She would be up early to get the kids off to school. Then Pop was there to make sure dinner was on the table while Carmen's mother worked nights on assembly and packing lines.

Carmen's mother and father came from Puerto Rico with limited education. Taking on a second job as a security guard, Pop told his children, "I will work as hard as I have to so that you all graduate from college." Over the years, his delivery route resulted in arthritis and asthma episodes, particularly in the cold. At seventy-six years old, his lungs hurt, but he had gotten his wish: all of his children were college graduates and Carmen was not only educated at the doctoral level, she was committed to furthering the education of others. Knowing that the equity vision she had shared with Dr. Harper at District 202 was now embedded in that district's curriculum and five-year plan, Carmen searched out other leadership and growth opportunities in 2011. She served on numerous statewide policy committees addressing the issues of unconscious bias within schools impacting the success of children of color. Her passion for the education of children, especially those who would otherwise be marginalized or excluded, led her to seek out another leadership role, this time as superintendent.

In late 2011, she interviewed with Berwyn North, was screened, and then was selected as one of six applicants to be interviewed by the board of education. In March of 2012, while sitting in her office at District 202, Carmen received a phone call.

"My heart was racing, and my palms were sweaty," she remembered. "When I was told the school board had made their selection and that they were going to be contacting me to offer me the position, I thought, Oh my God, this is happening."

She remembered the first superintendent she worked for, Dr. Charles Ponquinette—the first Black superintendent in his school district. So many years ago, he sat her down and said, "Carmen, no matter what decision you make—as long as you make that decision with the best interest of the children in mind—you will never go wrong."

Feeling a jumble of emotions running through her after hearing the news, Carmen hung up the phone, closed her eyes, thanked the good Lord for this opportunity, and prayed that He would guide her to make the right decisions for the children at Berwyn North. Then she let out a scream.

Knowing she could be effective in the role of superintendent, that she had a school board eager to see all their children excel, and that she could make a difference in the lives of the students and families within the district, she accepted the position.

Berwyn North District 98 reflected her own upbringing and culture. It was approximately 82 percent Latino and about 11 percent Black. However, she would be working with a primarily White administration and teaching staff.

Plainfield 202 and Berwyn North 98 differed in many significant ways. Plainfield 202 was in an area with a rapidly expanding population with many ethnic groups. Berwyn North was an older, established, and stable community that was primarily Hispanic. There were other differences, too:

DISTRICT 202	DISTRICT 98
An area of 64 square miles	Densely populated 1-square mile area
29,000 students in 30 schools	3,200 students in 4 schools
Serves several suburban communities	Two school districts serving the city of Berwyn
40 miles southwest of Chicago	7 miles west of Chicago
58% White students	93% students of color
Unit consolidated PK–12 district	Elementary PK–8 district
All-White board of education	Racially/ethnically diverse board of education

Building on Lessons Learned at Plainfield District 202

Dr. Ayala was appointed to the position in March of 2012 but wouldn't officially begin as superintendent until July 1 of that year, giving her three months to learn more about District 98. Over those three months, the previous superintendent graciously spent many hours with Carmen. He made the entire district office available to her by providing the space, sharing names and positions, going over each person's responsibilities, and communicating the schedule of interviews Carmen had developed for the staff. It was this series of interviews that provided Carmen with certain foundational realities regarding the district:

- The racial balance of the student population had been changing while the curriculum had stagnated.
- The district's literacy materials were fourteen years old.
- Their technology was sorely outdated.
- They were using an antiquated assessment not aligned to the new Illinois Learning Standards.
- The staff were not yet being trained to teach to the Common Core Standards (although the new state assessment was just two years away).
- The district wasn't adhering to requirements of the English Learner Program to the degree that a freeze had been placed on district funds by the state board of education because of the district's unwillingness to comply with the program.

To the previous superintendent's credit, he was waiting to move forward with the new literacy materials and had slowed down the administrators' updating of the assessment so that Carmen could be involved in those decisions. As a result, she simultaneously felt gratitude for his approach to this transition, while also quickly feeling overwhelmed by decisions that needed to be made, many required by the state.

It was also during this time that Carmen learned the district had nearly zero debt, atypical of Illinois school districts. In fact, the district had $42 million in reserves and an annual budget of $32 million, meaning it could survive without revenue for more than a year. The district had been receiving the highest financial rating from the state, and any superintendent or business manager would have been proud of such a financial profile.

The financial position certainly explained why a freeze of funds might not create the necessary motivation for compliance with the English Learner Program. However, it was still challenging for Carmen to reconcile the cash position with the low achievement scores of students in the district and the lack of updated materials, technology, and poorly focused teacher professional development. Somehow the district had come to prioritize its cash position over these needs. Whether it was an intentional or subconscious decision, to Carmen, the result felt out of alignment with the needs of the students.

Another Storm: An Intentional One

Another concern arose when Carmen was made aware that Berwyn North was seen by many as a "closed" district, meaning there was not much interaction with community organizations or community agencies. Thus, few people knew what was going on, and, as a result, few questioned the district. While this offered the district autonomy, it also isolated the district from a diverse range of input and kept the community at arm's length.

Because of her background, Carmen possessed a unique lens from which to view the challenge of family involvement: that of a Latina who grew up in a home where many sacrifices were made so she and her siblings could receive an education. The district had about 82 percent Latino and 28 percent English learners, which meant many parents didn't speak English. The district was speaking to families in a language these families didn't understand, and then the district was understandably frustrated when they were met with silence. Carmen believed that most parents cared deeply about their children's education just as her own parents had. She also believed that the teachers and administrators cared deeply about the students' education. Both were true, and yet something was getting in the way of progress.

Additional clues were quickly stacking up:

- The high population of Black and Brown students was being served by a predominantly White administration and teaching staff.
- Support staff were made up of more Black and Latino employees,

many of whom expressed feeling treated as second-class citizens.

- There was a belief among some administrators and staff that students' native languages should not be used in the classroom.
- The district was requiring that Spanish-speaking families adapt to what was most comfortable for the administration by communicating predominantly in English.
- Most glaringly, the district was on the receiving end of a court decree from the Office for Civil Rights for one school where teachers, social workers, and supervisors had not stopped racial bullying from occurring.

Five Major Initiatives Emerge

After Carmen officially took over the position of superintendent on July 1, 2012, her three months of due diligence had resulted in a strategy organized around five central initiatives. She remembered a major lesson from her days at Plainfield District 202: limit your focus—keep it to no more than four to five things. These five central initiatives, collectively endorsed by the cabinet, became the focus around which the district would plan and operate, the basis for the five-year instructional plan adopted by the board of education. They represented the foundational stones upon which District 98 would create a learning environment for all its students.

1. *Curriculum Consistency:* Having had success with the Curriculum Leadership Institute (CLI) in prior districts, CLI was hired in 2012–2013 to begin the curriculum development process. A five-year curriculum development plan was established and work on the curriculum began immediately.
2. *English Learners:* At the same time, the district began working on compliance. The required transitional bilingual model was strengthened, and a teacher coordinator was elevated to director of English language learners. This was key for the district's future transitioning toward a dual-language program. All teachers were required to participate in sheltered instruction observation protocol (SIOP) training, a specific training designed to make curriculum more accessible to students.

3. *Special Education:* The district had already begun piloting an inclusion instructional model that provided special education students access to general education. This model was intended to span all grades, kindergarten through eighth grade.

4. *Technology:* The district was struggling with technology and experiencing criticism from the community. The neighboring district had just implemented a 1:1 initiative where all its students received an Apple iPad. But before embarking on a large-scale purchase and implementation of that magnitude, a technology audit was conducted. The audit evaluated the current infrastructure leading to improvements in the state of technology. A technology plan was formulated and implemented to address the needs of the students in District 98.

5. *Cultural Responsiveness:* Woven throughout the other initiatives were many activities designed to address the theme of unconscious bias. Because of the dichotomy of a principally White staff teaching predominantly Hispanic and Black students, the initiative focused first on helping teachers identify and address cultural disconnections through cultural responsiveness training. The process began by training the leaders to train the teachers so the teachers could create a more inclusive learning environment.

Beginning with the Cultural Audit Data

As Carmen's plan shifted from idea to execution, she expected that teachers and administrators were going to be upset by the changes she would be implementing and the speed with which she would need to act, particularly in relation to state requirements. She was highly in tune with the human elements of change from her experience at District 202, while she also knew that legitimate data would provide further clarification and bolster the credibility of her decisions.

In the fall of 2012, Carmen brought in Bea Young Associates (BYA) to conduct an internal cultural audit at Berwyn North District 98. Using the BYA Educational Equity Journey model, Bea first conducted individual interviews with all board members, district office staff, principals, and assistant principals. She then followed up those interviews with homogeneous focus groups, including a cross-section of teaching staff, support staff, and students. Then, during spring 2013, an external audit was performed through individual interviews conducted with community leaders and homogeneous focus groups of parents.

As the sample quotes below demonstrate, responses to the internal and external audits revealed critical information, particularly around the issues of diversity and cultural responsiveness:

- *"We have shoved diversity under the carpet for a long time."* (White teacher)
- *"The importance of this topic is magnified due to the change in demographics of the district."* (board of education member)
- *"This initiative will bring everyone in the district closer."* (Hispanic non-certified staff)
- *"The handwriting is on the wall. It's time to embrace, incorporate, and teach diversity and be good examples to the students."* (Hispanic administrator)
- *"Finally, we will meet the changing needs of our students."* (Black non-certified staff)

Another area identified was the desire to hire more diverse teaching staff. There was a general sense that children needed more role models who reflected their culture and looked like them. Yet, finding a way forward brought up a range of different viewpoints, as illustrated below:

- *"Must find the qualified person; race and ethnicity is not a priority."* (board of education member)
- *"It is important to have Hispanic candidates, and it is good for our relations with the Hispanic community."* (board of education member)
- *"We cannot lower standards and hire for color."* (District leader)
- *"Not enough role models for African American and Latino students."* (African American support staff)

Many of the same themes were echoed in the external audit. Principle among them was the positive response that the district was embarking upon a journey to create an inclusive environment in which all its children could thrive. There were four major themes underscored by community leaders:

1. Valuing cultural differences at District 98 would make a difference and was overdue.
2. Enabling dialogue with the larger community was welcome.
3. Understanding the importance of role models, mentors, and staff of color was important.
4. Creating more multicultural events for the school and community was needed.

Parents' responses were similarly positive in relation to the district taking steps to become more inclusive and culturally responsive to their children. There were six major areas upon which they focused:

1. Pride in the new direction of District 98 and the quality of its teachers
2. Need for more parental involvement, especially for parents of color
3. Lack of communication and discomfort with conversations about multiculturalism
4. Desire to build cultural differences into the curriculum
5. Hope to create more proactive communications about cultural connections within the schools and the community at large
6. Acknowledgment that not only Black and Hispanic parents felt excluded, but the same was true for White parents who spoke only English (This was a unique insight into all dimensions of diversity throughout the district at the time.)

Responding to Resistance

On the flip side, the audit also identified some resentment and resistance. In February of 2013, all district staff participated in a diversity and cultural responsiveness workshop that included a review of the results of the internal audit and ended with an evaluation form that posed two questions. Respondents were asked to indicate if they strongly agreed, agreed, were neutral, disagreed, or strongly disagreed with the following two statements: 1) I am aware of the results of the internal cultural diversity audit; and 2) I understand the role of inclusive behaviors to enhance the ability to create cultural change. Of the 217 evaluations, 209 responded either "strongly agree" or "agree." Six individuals were neutral. Two disagreed.

Forty-five written comments were also collected, of which thirty-nine were positive and six were moderately negative to extremely negative.

Through subsequent dialogue, it was revealed that some White teachers felt they were not being valued, that they were being disrespected. Some feared losing their jobs and being replaced by teachers of color and Spanish-speaking faculty. While Carmen continued to reinforce that no one was going to lose their job because they didn't speak Spanish or were not a person of color, she also knew that she was coming into the district as a relatively unknown entity, was making significant changes, and—while many were state required—was still seen as the "disruptor."

Carmen had witnessed firsthand how change within a system forces people to feel emotions they didn't necessarily ask for or want to feel. She knew when people perceived an aspect of their life being threatened, it was normal to downshift on Maslow's hierarchy,[6] in which case behavior could be exhibited from fight or flight mode. For some within the system, Carmen's arrival was enhancing their sense of safety, while for others, their sense of safety seemingly felt diminished. Carmen focused on the importance of not blaming people for the behavior they might exhibit when they felt unsafe. Instead, her goal was to reserve judgment as best she could, honor where people were, offer clarity when possible, and help them shift into alignment with the vision.

A challenge Carmen was forced to face is that human beings often become upset or spiral as they feel less and less safe. When anyone spirals downward, it becomes challenging to take a self-actualized look inward at what is occurring. Instead, human nature is to look outward to fix "the problem" and reestablish a sense of control. As the individual disrupting the system, Carmen was viewed by some as "that problem to be fixed."

One such individual expressed anger through a series of anonymous letters sent to board members. The first raised the concern that Carmen and Bea Young working together on the audit presented a conflict of interest because Carmen was featured on the BYA website and because Carmen and Bea were writing a book to share the results of their work together in District 202. The letter ended with the statement, "I am a

6   A. H. Maslow, "A Theory of Human Motivation," *Psychological Review*, 50, no. 4 (1943): 370–96.

person who believes in speaking out, and sending an unsigned letter feels bad, but I want to protect a much-loved job." The letter was signed "Whistleblower."

The second anonymous letter was addressed to the school board president and shared that "People seem to be buying into Dr. Ayala's agenda, and that scares those of us who see her agenda as self-serving rather than for the good of this district and the students in the district."

> ... the internal cultural audit was not conducted to place blame but to gain awareness of how staff and students felt.

The third letter expressed embarrassment that the district asked parents and community members to participate in the cultural audit, stating that "Many of us have worked with all of our students for many years, meeting the needs of our students and families, and we love our jobs. Instead of applauding our accomplishments and encouraging us to build on them, Superintendent Ayala has shamed us by labeling us racist."

In a demonstration of support for Carmen, the school board took the position that any grievance submitted would only be given time and consideration if the sender included their name so that a substantive conversation could be had. The board's support was invaluable; still, the feedback was challenging to receive. Carmen felt it was important to strike a fine line and remain firm in her messaging while not blaming anyone who was reacting angrily to the direction she was moving the district.

Because the next all-staff meeting was a month away, she penned a letter to her colleagues to emphasize that no person had or ever would lose their job because of the color of their skin. Nor would any person be hired simply because of the color of their skin. She reminded everyone of her committee approach to hiring and that committee members participated in reference checks on candidates. She emphasized that the internal cultural audit was not conducted to place blame but to gain awareness of how staff and students felt. Addressing her affiliation with Bea Young, she shared that the Illinois Education Association's legal counsel looked into the allegation and determined there was no legal or financial conflict of interest. Lastly, she invited her colleagues to work with her, to bring forward ideas, to respectfully share opinions, and to call and send emails with thoughts on how, together, they could "uncover, dispel, address, and improve what we are here for . . . the education of all our students." The final words on her letter were "my door is open."

Of course, the anonymous letters were not the first pushback Carmen experienced since she was offered the position of superintendent. Starting in July, Carmen established the cabinet of administrators at the district level who would have responsibilities across all four schools. One of the four principals had applied for the position of superintendent, and when that principal was not selected, some of those who knew and supported her understandably viewed Carmen in an unfavorable light. Additionally, one of the assistant superintendents who applied for the superintendent position abandoned her position when she was not hired, bringing the entire curriculum and instruction area of the district to a halt.

Thankfully, each single challenging response to Carmen and to the changes she was making was counterbalanced by multiple voices of appreciation. Carmen received an overwhelmingly positive number of responses to the all-staff letter she wrote. A handful are shared below:

> "I have never felt so welcome to share my ideas, thoughts, opinions, and concerns."

> "Bravo . . ."

> "We needed this audit . . . I found nothing offensive about the workshop . . . it made me reflect on my own biases and blind spots."

> "I found the audit to be enlightening and forward-thinking."

> "You have my support, as I believe you when you say you have the best interests of the students of District 98 at heart."

> "Please know there are many of us out here who applaud your efforts, who know that your intentions are the best, and [who] will support your efforts to do what is best for our students."

". . . you are the best thing that has happened in this district in the [thirteen] years I have worked here."

Moving Forward with Inclusive Behaviors

Based on learnings from both the internal and the external cultural audits, a committee known as "Berwyn North Building Bridges," or BNB[2], was developed to formalize cultural responsiveness within the district's school and community environment and thus make it more systemic. Work had been done to engage staff and community on the issues of cultural responsiveness. The model for these conversations became the five inclusive behaviors, as shown in the following:

This poster is displayed in every school within District 98 to help reinforce the district's educational equity journey. It is used by principals and assistant principals as a reminder of the cultural responsiveness professional development teachers received beginning in 2015, and it continues today. Importantly, it is used as a reference when situations occur in classrooms or offices that potentially can break down communication among individuals or groups. Utilizing the inclusive behaviors is one part of helping staff understand that cultural responsiveness requires ongoing, sometimes daily, conversations.

Some of the steps at Berwyn North District 98 that differed from Plainfield District 202 included the following:

- Cultural responsiveness training was conducted during one of Dr. Ayala's first institute days, with the entire BYA team conducting workshops for small groups of teachers, secretaries, and custodians.
- Inclusive behaviors training was given in 2014–15 for principals, assistant principals, and the administrative cabinet.
- A train-the-trainer model for the inclusive behaviors training was developed to address the theme of unconscious bias. Principals, assistant principals, central office administrators, and key district staff were certified by BYA so that they could teach teachers. Teachers would then teach students. Unlike District 202's approach, this training is ongoing at Berwyn North.

> ... cultural responsiveness requires ongoing, sometimes daily, conversations.

The train-the-trainer approach offered two primary benefits in contrast to external consultant training. First, it represented a cost savings for the district, and, even more importantly, principals and administrators not only became trainers but also learned to lead by example, which embedded an inclusive environment within the district's culture.

As a follow-up to this training, Carmen developed and pursued ongoing professional cultural responsiveness dialogues. These conversations were applied in practical, day-to-day ways as administrators and teachers were asked to heighten their awareness of situations of unconscious bias that might exist within the schools.

Carmen also made a practice of regularly touring and observing the four schools within her district to look for opportunities to coach and challenge the trainers. On one such visit to several classrooms in one school, she noticed several instances where individual Black students were physically separated from the rest of the students. She shared her observation with the school's principal and participating teachers and with her administrative team. Because the separation appeared to be a pattern within the school, it had become a blind spot. This observation became the basis for helping her internal team open up a conversation around how bias plays out in subtle ways, reinforcing the statement that sometimes we don't see all of what we see.

Grounding District 98's Change Effort in Cultural Responsiveness

As with Plainfield District 202, the Cultural Responsiveness Curriculum model below was an integral part of building curriculum throughout the district while meeting the requirements of Illinois state standards.

What was different from District 202 was that each SAC was given additional training and content around how to build curriculum. The subject matter alone was not the only target; it was imperative that the curriculum be culturally relevant to the district's diverse students.

> The subject matter alone was not the only target; it was imperative that the curriculum be culturally relevant to the district's diverse students.

Culturally focused material was provided by Susan O'Halloran, a BYA senior associate who created a cultural responsiveness workshop for each of the district's SACs beginning in 2013–14. As subject area materials are now updated regularly, this remains an ongoing process. The components of O'Halloran's approach to creating culturally responsive curriculum are summarized in the following graphic and expanded in chapter 6:

Components of Culturally Responsive Curriculum

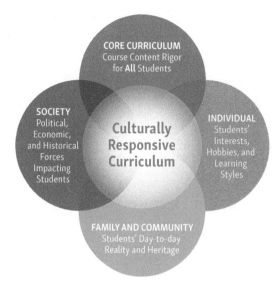

CORE CURRICULUM—Is curriculum content developed by subject matter experts convened throughout the district? Is the curriculum aligned horizontally and vertically for each grade level within the district?

INDIVIDUAL—Are resources and time provided for educators to learn about individual students and how they learn?

FAMILY AND COMMUNITY—Is subject matter reflective of students' home cultures? Are educators encouraged to reflect on their own cultural lens to look at subject matter differently?

SOCIETY—Does the subject matter show you care about the world in which your students live and empower them to be active members of society?

Whenever a student can say "YES! This subject is about me, my family, and my world," that's the aim of a culturally responsive curriculum.

© 2017 Susan O'Halloran

As with the inclusive behaviors training, the work continues within the SACs today through many ongoing workshops and conversations about cultural responsiveness.

Measuring Achievement Results

In 2016, four years after Carmen took over as superintendent and began the implementation of her strategy, preliminary results from the new state assessment showed that District 98 scores were beginning to surpass neighboring districts for the very first time.

Fulfilling the English Learner Program requirements, information was provided to families in both English and Spanish, resulting in a bilingual website, bilingual district and school newsletters, and bilingual marquee messages as the norm in District 98. Regarding special education, during 2016, the district had a higher percentage of special education students than the state average. To address this, a revision to the intervention process took place to promote collaboration and sharing between departments formerly operating as silos. Rather than a separate curriculum, as was offered in the past, special education teachers and students were beginning to be included in the general classroom.

Students in District 98 demonstrate a culturally responsive math lesson at a school board meeting.

Achievement Results at District 98[7]

PARCC DATA: FOUR YEARS OF PROGRESS

	Composite 2015	Composite 2016	Composite 2017	Composite 2018	Difference
District 98	**23**	**29**	**32**	**42**	**+19**
District V	21	23	21	25	+4
District W	11	12	15	17	+6
District X	21	22	23	26	+5
District Y	21	23	25	36	+15
District Z	59	52	49	41	–18
State	33	34	34	37	+4

Data collected for Berwyn North is state assessment data. Unlike the data provided for District 202, here the state changed its assessment to align to the Common Core. Instead of the ISATs, Illinois adopted in

---

7   Illinois School Report Card Data, https://www.isbe.net/pages/illinois-state-report-card -data.aspx.

2014 the Partnership for Assessment of Readiness for College and Career (PARCC) as the test to measure student achievement.

An achievement gap analysis between the district and the state, using data from the 2013 state assessment, showed a difference of 11 percentage points between the state and the district. By 2018, that difference had shifted to District 98 surpassing the state by 4 percentage points in reading. In math, the difference in 2013 was 15 percentage points. By 2018, this had been reduced to 6 percentage points.

As of 2018, PARCC had been administered for several years and was showing achievement improvement of various groups. Separating the data by groups of students demonstrated that overall students had gained 10 percentage points between 2015 and 2018. Black students gained 7 percentage points, Hispanics 12 percentage points, low-income 12 points, and English learners 8 points. Achievement gaps also reflect positive shifts. Report card data also shows that the White/Black achievement gap in District 98 was 22 (Berwyn) and 28 (Illinois) in 2015. By 2018 the data indicated that the gap was 9 (Berwyn) and 29 (Illinois). Berwyn District 98's gap between Black/White students has since been reduced by 13 percentage points while Illinois' has increased 1 percentage point.

A comparison with five other districts feeding into the local high school was also performed. District 98 was the only district of the five that showed a gain in reading. In math, District 98 had the greatest gains of the four schools feeding into the local high school and the highest percentage of students meeting standards.

No one in District 98 could remember a time when students in the district had outperformed their counterparts in the other feeder districts in either reading or math. Berwyn North had surpassed them in both.

It is also worth noting that District 98, at the time of this writing, still operates debt-free. The district's cash position is not the same, however; with Carmen as superintendent, the district's fund balances have increased even as the improvements had been implemented.

Two Systemic Processes Close the Gap . . . Again

Any initiative is only as good as the results it produces. The success Berwyn North District 98 has experienced is just as magnificent as that experienced previously at Plainfield 202. The lesson here is that the Educational Equity Journey and the CLI models, applied intentionally, can be effective in school districts with great variances in size and demographics of the student population. It is a replicable and reliable way of closing the achievement gap.

There are two major differences to which Carmen attributes the positive results at District 98:

1. An emphasis on building a personal understanding of the district's overall culture before officially becoming superintendent
2. Building an understanding about cultural responsiveness among board members and school leaders at the outset through the internal cultural audit

Thinking back on her first year at District 98, Carmen reflected, "At Plainfield District 202, as we addressed cultural storms within the district, I became known as the 'change pain.' At Berwyn North District 98, I didn't have the luxury of waiting for the storm to come to me. I had to become 'the storm' to improve the quality of education the children were receiving."

"Cultural Responsiveness is the plate upon which the success of everything rests," observed Carmen in relation to both District 202 and District 98. "Given that teachers at District 98 were primarily White, working with children who were primarily Hispanic and Black, we had to build cultural responsiveness while taking on the task of rebuilding the curriculum."

> Cultural Responsiveness is the plate upon which the success of everything rests.

Happily, we end this chapter on a celebratory note. With a student body of 95 percent children of color and 90 percent children coming from homes with limited resources, we did it! Under the state's new ESSA accountability plan, Lincoln Middle School, within District 98, was designated as "exemplary." With almost four thousand schools in Illinois, only the top 10 percent meeting criteria are designated as "exemplary." We celebrate collaboration. We celebrate community coming together. We celebrate potential. There has been a lot of work by teachers, administrators, support staff, parents, and especially students. There is no question. A deliberate focus on equity and cultural responsiveness has closed gaps and led to academic excellence.

3   LESSONS LEARNED

It Takes Leadership, Collaboration, and Soul

"We're doing Dr. King's work. I think he would approve our celebrating his birthday this way," proclaimed Bea as she planned our writing team retreat for the long Martin Luther King holiday weekend in January 2018. Having just escaped the wicked Chicago cold, she was opening her South Florida condominium in anticipation of the team's time together.

Much of this book had been created with conference calls, countless emails, and virtual online editing technology. Writing in three different locations, separated by thousands of miles, had been amazing—and frustrating. Given locations and work commitments, Google Docs had been the "go-to" tool to keep the manuscript progressing. Yet, nuances of meaning, that can only be caught in the light of another person's eye when reading aloud, are lost in a virtual office with three cursors moving across a computer screen. Finding time together to share ideas, face-to-face, was a cherished occasion.

The MLK weekend retreat in Naples had been etched in stone on our collective calendars for several months. Then came the phone call from Carmen, who, as we were gathering, was stranded in the Chicago area. "I'm not sure if I can make it. Temps plunged to seven degrees yesterday morning. Every building in the district has cracked pipes. Contractors are standing outside my office. Assuming we can get them fixed, there's a lake effect storm on the way. Flights are being canceled as I speak."

Storms have a way of punctuating our story.

Despite the odds, Carmen handled the emergencies and caught a flight a day later. Our team was whole again.

As we began our MLK weekend retreat, we remembered how Dr. King was the first to speak the phrase "the fierce urgency of now" in his legendary "I Have a Dream" speech. Over fifty-five years later, that sense of "urgency" is driving educators when considering the issues of educational equity.

The achievement gap had been well documented by the 1966 Coleman Report, yet there had been little to no improvement over the ensuing decades. The passage of No Child Left Behind in 2001 attempted to address these disparities by creating consequences. Yet they provided no clear way forward to close the gap. The national conversation began to change in 2013 when USDE Secretary of Education Arne Duncan created the Equity and Excellence Commission, a group of educational experts, economists, and civil rights leaders. They issued a report called *For Each and Every Child: A Strategy for Education Equity and Excellence*, which outlined a policy framework for closing what the commission called the "education gap."

In any given month there are many conferences, both local and national, focused on educational equity. Books, ranging from school law to pedagogy to curriculum, show dozens of titles with the word "equity" included. Journal articles number in the hundreds. Many offer a diagnosis of what ails American education. Few offer proven solutions. And here we were in January 2018 finishing the stories of Districts 202 and 98 where the achievement gap actually closed. It's our fervent belief this book answers Dr. King's urgent call of "now" with demonstrable results and a replicable approach.

> It's our fervent belief this book answers Dr. King's urgent call of "now" with demonstrable results and a replicable approach.

We had two major tasks during our warm Florida gathering time. The first was to review our first two chapters that demonstrated the equity success stories, putting each under the microscopes of clarity and compelling storytelling. The second was to distill more than ten years of experience—garnered in these two districts—into lessons learned.

What worked? What could have been done differently? Where did we miss the mark? What kept us going? Were there non-negotiables? What had we learned that could help others who might consider embarking on this journey?

This "Lessons Learned" chapter intends to take stock of what was necessary to create a successful, sustainable educational equity change effort in these two Illinois school districts and what might have been done differently. Before we provide the "how-to" tools in part II, it's our intent that the next few pages will provide readers with enough information to understand the breadth and depth of what is involved when creating an environment where the gaps in academic achievement can be closed.

Creating an environment that supports the systems required for educational equity is a human enterprise. The successes of District 202 and District 98 were a confluence of 1) principled, solution-oriented, and knowledgeable leaders; 2) external guidance; 3) dedicated teachers; and 4) children and families who did the hard work. Our story is about the right people coming together at the right time. Yet, at its core, it's about school leaders willing to take risks. Those risks can come at a cost . . . which is where we begin our "lessons learned."

1. Achieving educational equity can come at a personal cost and yet can become your legacy.

For anyone considering closing the achievement gap, it's important to note that building a culturally responsive school environment is going to be key, and that it may come at some personal cost. "This is especially true," Carmen said, "when organizations go the route of hiring one person of color in a higher-level position to direct the initiative."

> . . . at its core, it's about school leaders willing to take risks. Those risks can come at a cost . . .

As a Latina, Carmen had experienced the cost of cultural change in especially personal, demeaning ways. There was the unusual situation, where the District 202 Board of Education went outside the chain of command to evaluate her performance, creating what Carmen referred to as "the most painful experience of [her] career." As the lone person of color, Carmen became the one to shoulder all the issues of race, culture, language, and cultural responsiveness.

She remembers: "At District 202, John was my support, and he knew everything I went through. In Berwyn, when teachers were angry, the board took a stand. We need to acknowledge the frustration, stress, attacks, and bias, both conscious and unconscious, that a person of color endures when they are in an accountability position when a school system is pursuing greater educational equity. Without support, this person will justifiably burn out."

"Even though District 98 had a clear, focused, inclusive, well-communicated plan, I was called the 'disruptor,'" Carmen continued. "Hearing that about myself was hard even when I realized it was said out of fear of the change efforts."

Bea responded, "I've often seen this—where leaders of color are held to a higher standard—referred to as a 'double standard.' We Whites, looking through the lens of our privilege, don't understand the impact and often deny the personal cost Carmen is describing."

Added Carmen, "I was blessed to have Bea talk me off a ledge on more than one occasion. Having outside expertise and perspective to guide the process can make all the difference. This is not an easy thing to do even in the best of situations."

Regardless of the race or gender, the pressure of being the leader can be intense.

"I'll never forget the day I walked into Dr. Harper's office and he was modifying his entire five-year plan to incorporate learnings from the cultural audit," Bea recalled. "At that point, I knew all the work we'd done would make a difference. Looking up, he said, 'My tombstone will read, *Equity killed me.*' I suggested a revision to his perspective by asserting, 'No, John; it will read, *Equity was my legacy.*'"

Tom Hernandez, the Plainfield director of community relations, had said in an interview, "to take on this kind of change effort has enormous costs—personally, culturally, politically. In the big scheme of things, it doesn't cost a lot financially; but you have to be prepared for failures, and you have to expect pushback."

2. It's a journey, not a quick fix.

Thinking about our own experiences, the theme of "go slow" was continually reinforced, particularly to remind us there are reasons things are the way they are within any given school district and its surrounding community. It was critical that superintendents, school leaders, or outside consultants did not impugn the motives or values of people in the schools or community. People who felt judged were often sent into fight or flight survival mode when they thought their jobs or children's futures were at stake. That is not a place from which to make collaborative and transformative decisions, so we had to work hard not to blame others. That can be a challenge since, as Tom Hernandez, puts it, "The public education system abhors change. We try to kill flies with cannons."

Given the rapid growth at Plainfield District 202, going slow, however, rarely felt like an option. And the speed of change came with costs. In Dr. Harper's words, "In hindsight I would have spent more time laying the groundwork for this process. Perhaps another way of saying this would be to tell staff and the board of education, 'Prepare yourself for things you may not want to hear.'"

Thinking back to District 202, Carmen added, "Go slow—the biggest complaint we received was the amount of change we were undertaking over a short period. I was known as the 'change pain' for a while."

"Yes," allowed Bea. "It's critical to prepare yourself and your community. Examine carefully the history, size, and demographics of the district. Learn what resources you can depend on—where the resistance may show up. Get to know the politics of the community as well as the school. That way you can better equip stakeholders to know what's coming—in a way they can hear. When those resistances show up, call them out as a reminder to everyone: 'Remember, we knew this was coming; everybody, take a deep breath.'"

"I was able to do that at District 98," said Carmen. "Because of the three months spent learning about the district prior to becoming superintendent, I was able to build approval and support. I used the time to create a list of challenge points to guide the changes and to limit the changes to the few which I believed would create the greatest impact. My advice to anyone in this role is to choose your focus—limit your priorities to no more than four or five."

3. Listen to the resistance and trust the principles behind the systemic process.

Students and teachers successfully closed the achievement gap at both districts in our story, using two intertwined models to guide the process. The Educational Equity Journey model and the CLI model were both necessary to the change effort. Both required expertise, intention, perseverance, and faith since neither on its own is sufficient.

The educational equity journey model guided the overarching organizational change, while the CLI model provided the nuts and bolts of creating curriculum that was both horizontally and vertically aligned, something rare in most school districts. A reminder: aligning the curriculum horizontally means that all similar grades teach the same curriculum, while aligning vertically means there is a continuation from one grade level to the next.

"Curriculum is the backbone. It's what we teach," asserted Carmen in an interview. "Having a rigorous, articulated, and aligned curriculum is a non-negotiable."

She continued: "The CLI approach by itself isn't enough, however. By layering in the Educational Equity Journey, a culturally responsive environment is created, one in which all children feel valued. Cultural responsiveness is about the relationships that people in the organization bring to the process and is something we want all our children to learn."

> We need to honor resistance because within the resistance is also the motivation for change.

"Absolutely. Use the models and trust the process," exclaimed Bea. "Listen to the resistance. Respond to it and trust the response to resistance is built into the Educational Equity Journey model. We need to honor resistance because within the resistance is also the motivation for change."

Behind the Educational Equity Journey and the CLI model are a set of principles that guide the process. They are not a set of best practices nor a specific teaching methodology.

Instead, both approaches seek to identify context-specific reforms based on a district's needs. At their heart they are about building relationships within a district that empower administrators, support staff, teachers, students, and families.

4. The cultural audit data does the convincing of the need for change.

Transparency of communication is required throughout the process of creating cultural change. Conducting anonymous assessments of a cross-section of the district's stakeholders can provide the necessary insights to create the most effective plan of action.

"Conducting internal and external cultural audits is the first step in raising awareness of the need for cultural change within the district," according to Bea. "These audits are part of our proven model because the data does the convincing." Sharing the audit data becomes a key process to clarifying why problems arose as well as what opportunities may exist with the district or community to change procedures, rules, and perhaps even norms.

For Carmen, "Information from the internal and external audits helped to identify areas of improvement in both school districts. Communication about the audit needs to be done systematically and over the long term because gathering and sharing data by itself aren't enough to sustain the journey. Cultural responsiveness is not a one-time workshop or institute day event, but an investment that must be based on the district's current culture with a vision for its future. Success requires ongoing professional development and conversations with all staff on issues that impact the district's performance. Communication about cultural responsiveness isn't only about reporting the findings of the cultural audit. On an ongoing basis, I observed the impacts of changes we've implemented and continued to ask for feedback to keep us or get us back on track."

5. Commitment and vision need to be shared by all.

At the core of the educational equity journey is the necessity to create a leadership commitment. A vision, held in common by the board of education, administrative staff, teacher leaders, and community leaders, underpins the journey. It informs every step of the process.

Accordingly, Bea advises: "Take time to learn the dynamics of the leadership structure, at both the elected and staff level. This journey is best made when there's a clear vision shared by all leaders."

Mike Kelly's voice from ten years ago echoed in our minds when thinking about the central role of leadership: "My advice is to keep your focus on what is good for all the kids. Don't try to fix things that have nothing to do with education. It's about the kids."

Tom Hernandez shared the same idea thinking back about the Illinois School Journal article entitled "The Magnificent Story of District 202": "You have to stay focused on the vision—the prize—seeing all children served by the district's policies and practices."

6. Recognize and address implicit institutional bias.

One example of institutional bias in our story was the Plainfield District 202 Freshman Academy. By segregating so many young men of color, it created an environment of lower expectations for both the staff and the students. Without intending to, simply by being placed in the Academy, students got the demeaning message, "You don't have a chance." This recalls the message that described the rationale for President George W. Bush in creating NCLB in 2001; the lack of high standards for all students created "the soft bigotry of low expectations." The Freshman Academy stood as an example of "low expectations."

"Because of John's concern about the disproportionate levels of discipline meted out to Black kids," remembered Bea, "we were able to score an early win for educational equity at District 202. When he disbanded the Freshman Academy, it sent a clear message to everyone in the district that his equity vision did indeed include all students. Just as Ryan's banter in the hallway kept him off the basketball team until Dr. Harper intervened, the Academy had reinforced the perception that Black and Hispanic kids are the problem."

"I saw another kind of institutional bias based not on race but on an academic discipline," stated Carmen. "Special education teachers need to have additional endorsements on their license. The teachers and their students tend to work in silos apart from the rest of the school. I found that to be the case when I became superintendent at Berwyn North. I'm challenging that model and am committed to mainstreaming these children into the regular classrooms."

Carmen went on to explain that the "pull-out" approach for students with special needs denies them a full classroom experience. Though the intent is to provide special services, an unintended impact by differentiating these students is to lower academic rigor and create "low expectations."

She also reminded us of the recent tour she made where there appeared to be a pattern of Black students sitting and working separately from all the other children. As our story pointed out earlier, this had become a blind spot for principals and teachers alike. Carmen's observation became the basis for helping her staff open a conversation about how bias occurs in subtle ways—yet another example of how the "soft bigotry of low expectations" plays out.

7. Build cultural responsiveness through collaborative relationships.

The professional relationship between superintendent and principal is complicated. The superintendent is dependent upon the principal to implement the district's equity vision in each building. However, principals may experience pushback from teachers, students, and parents alike. Not surprisingly, there's a temptation to let teachers go about their business in order to maintain peace in the schools.

That's where the premise of the educational equity journey comes into play. If principals have had a role in creating the district's equity vision, they are more inclined to own the vision with their superintendent. Similarly, if teachers have a central role in creating the curriculum, they are invested in making it work. The model works because it builds collaborative relationships.

Though it exists as the proverbial double-edged sword, the superintendent's position does come with power. During our conversation, Carmen asserted, "You have to utilize the power of your position. Your leadership can make a difference; but you also must include others in the change process."

"There are days when I'd like to snap my fingers to see everyone magically on board," dreamed Carmen. "It doesn't work that way. My role has many facets—boss, problem-solver, budget analyst, communicator, coach, team player, mentor, and professional educator—just to name a few. The core component of each role is building and sustaining relationships. To keep those relationships true, one of the other non-negotiables I've learned from Bea is to utilize inclusive behaviors."

> ... for every exclusive behavior there's an inclusive behavior that can build effective, working relationships.

Bea agreed. "In complex school organizations where conflicting agendas are common, it isn't unusual for many to feel like outsiders. There's a dynamic of exclusion that exists whenever there are insiders and outsiders. The signs are there; yet for every exclusive behavior there's an inclusive behavior that can build effective, working relationships."

8. Challenge exclusion by utilizing inclusive behaviors.

Part II of our book is devoted to giving you, our reader, examples of how our principles, conceptual models, and practical tools were applied to achieve educational equity. Although chapter 5 of part II is devoted to the topic of inclusive behaviors, inclusivity is such an important part of building relationships and cultural responsiveness, we made it part of our "lessons learned." Our experience demonstrates that inclusivity is an imperative aspect of the educational equity journey.

"One of the reasons that closing the achievement gap moved more quickly at District 98," said Carmen, "is that we provided ongoing inclusive behaviors professional development beginning early in my tenure. Principals were certified in this process, so it became part of their role, not only to teach the course but, just as importantly, to model and reinforce those behaviors in staff meetings and with teachers in the classrooms."

"Certain behaviors exist within a community for many historic reasons," stated Bea. "Thus, the importance of utilizing non-blaming statements is underscored when talking about any issue. Work to understand the impacts of the change you are creating and how those changes might be received within each level of the organization. And reserve your judgments by reminding yourself that any resistance you perceive is a human being trying to grapple with change that feels counterintuitive to what their own life experience has shown them."

"Value, appreciate, and utilize inclusive language," Bea added. "For educators, inclusive language is often the key to actual behavior change with both colleagues and students."

9. Measure and share success openly.

As we reported at Plainfield District 202, the district's ability to measure its success against state standards changed the organizational narrative from one of discord to one of pride, which is sustained even today. Dr. Harper affirmed, "The ability to measure change is critical. Metrics and data can drive the process."

Board President Mike Kelly remembered: "In moving from being a failing school system to closing the gap for all children in the district, we were, in some cases, exceeding the success of our neighboring districts, which had more resources. Seeing those numbers turned the tide for many on the board."

Superintendent John Harper recognized the positive shift not only in the numbers, but also in how the district's culture was changing. As he stated in chapter 1, "I began to see the huge resistance from the teachers slowly turn from negativity to acceptance to embracing the process. They became a learning community. Seeing them begin to feel empowered let me know it was worth the effort."

10. We often don't know what we don't know.

Bea recalled years later a setback at District 98 when her team didn't provide the appropriate groundwork for the cultural audit feedback. "We had done it differently at District 202. Instead of beginning with the audit results, we began with an introduction to diversity and inclusion. It was a lively experience, which allowed staff to learn about cultural responsiveness in a way that prepared them for what was coming. Communicating and educating first about cultural awareness helped build ownership and created confidence in the educational equity journey they were soon to experience. Groups need to learn first what they 'don't know they don't know' in a non-threatening, inclusive learning setting. Lay the groundwork by first introducing the principles of diversity and cultural responsiveness."

"I was naïve about the state of race relations," remembered Dr. Harper. "I truly thought we'd advanced more in our society than we had. Even now it's clear that White people haven't come very far in terms of how we view 'those' people. A first step for anyone taking on this equity effort would be to educate themselves."

Bea added to this thought: "We must become aware of our own unconscious biases, then help others by modeling our change in behavior."

"No one, including John, had built a base for doing the work at District 202," stated former administrator Joan Woolwine. "Carmen was given carte blanche to go for it; but there wasn't a base of support. The miracle is that it continues today because of the strength of the process."

11. Enjoy your achievements.

Central to the educational equity journey is the vision held by leaders. In creating and carrying that vision to its completion, our two school superintendents and their teams faced and overcame extraordinary challenges personally and professionally. How did they do it? Where did they find the energy? We close this section with words from our story's key leaders about how they felt when it was evident their efforts had made a difference.

For Dr. Harper, "Beyond being able to show the measurable results, it came together for me when I saw most, if not all, teachers and administrators understood [that] the changes we made benefited all the children."

Carmen shared the following: "Seeing how the results of this collaboration impacts our students, makes all the fears and tears worth it. Creating a culturally responsive curriculum and learning community is an intensive professional development experience for administrators and teachers. Whenever the district staff become excited about what they teach, students 'get it' and become engaged."

All lessons are priceless when you experience the multitude of affirmations and achievements throughout the journey. Transformations occur at the leadership, teaching, support, student, and community levels. Seeing and feeling resistance turn into acceptance and support strengthens relationships at all levels. Finally, watching how students flourish and thrive when making academic gains and feeling included is when you know the "soul of education is being restored."

Embarking on an educational equity journey will inevitably come with its own series of lessons learned. We have attempted to identify commonalities between our two school district stories, which we believe will be helpful to other school organizations. While not in any order of importance, our Lessons Learned included the following:

- Achieving educational equity can come at a personal cost and yet can become your legacy.
- It's a journey, not a quick fix.
- Listen to the resistance and trust the principles behind the process.
- The cultural audit does the convincing of the need for change.
- Commitment and vision need to be shared by all.
- Recognize and address implicit institutional bias.
- Build cultural responsiveness through collaborative relationships.
- Challenge exclusion by utilizing inclusive behaviors.
- Measure and share success openly.
- We often don't know what we don't know.
- Enjoy your achievements.

PART II

What You Can Do: Tools to Take the Equity Journey

INTRODUCTION

Are You Ready? Personal and Organizational Assessments

"I am very angry at the feedback from the cultural audit presentation. So, because I'm a White woman, I don't show any students respect? I don't value my students' culture? You have just negated my years of dedicated service to this district. You don't know my background or my experience. You will now have teachers based on race, not quality? I am sick and tired of the 'woe is me' attitude! How about 'do something for yourself.' 'Strive for excellence.' I feel very disrespected."

—*A teacher's response after hearing the cultural audit feedback*

The quote above is an example of feedback you may hear. Thus, there is a need to assess initially where you stand personally and organizationally on these issues before you go on the journey. The challenging, yet exciting, journey to "restoring the soul to education" in your school system begins with you, the professional educator.

> **Do you worry about meeting the needs of ALL students?**

As an educator, you hear and attempt to balance your constituents' priorities. These play out at every conceivable level, especially when it seems that everyone or no one knows the "right" answer. In the policy debates and conflicts about resources, it's easy to forget that each group believes their actions best serve the needs of the students. But, before you begin, what drew you to this book?

- Have you been frustrated trying to close the achievement gap?
- Do you worry about meeting the needs of all students?

- Do you want to know more about how culture and race impact your students?
- Do you have a vision that you can't get others to understand?

You're in the middle. You have a set of beliefs and values about creating an environment in which students can thrive. In that sense, you know you have to lead your stakeholders. That's why you were called to this position. Simultaneously, you are surrounded by many voices, sometimes discordant, each needing to be heard. Thus, your skills as an educator, facilitator, arbitrator, and leader are critical to your success.

These roles require various sets of competencies. The following self-assessment is a tool to help evaluate your personal strengths and opportunities for improvement. Its intent is to give you a snapshot of how well-equipped you are for the equity journey.

PERSONAL EQUITY ASSESSMENT

Directions: For each question, rate yourself on a scale of 1 to 5 in terms of perceived proficiency, with 5 representing highest proficiency and 1 representing an area where you feel you need considerable work.

COMPETENCIES FOR EQUITY SUCCESS

A.	Do my words and actions inspire others to create an environment of excellence in which ALL students thrive?	1	2	3	4	5
B.	Do I understand the impact of my communication style on others?	1	2	3	4	5
C.	Do I encourage those with different communication styles, backgrounds, and perspectives to contribute their ideas in group settings?	1	2	3	4	5
D.	Do I take time to positively engage others who challenge my decisions?	1	2	3	4	5
E.	When faced with major decisions, do I search out the voices that are usually not included?	1	2	3	4	5
F.	Do I understand that my perspectives may be different than those in my communities?	1	2	3	4	5
G.	Do I seek opportunities to learn about the culture and backgrounds of others?	1	2	3	4	5
H.	When conflict exists across different cultures, do I create opportunities to find common ground?	1	2	3	4	5
I.	Do I understand my own biases and how my values may differ from the communities I serve?	1	2	3	4	5

REVIEW YOUR RESULTS

After you've completed your Personal Equity Assessment, take time to note what insights have surfaced. What might you do differently?

ORGANIZATIONAL EQUITY ASSESSMENT

This second assessment tool helps to evaluate an organization's preparedness for educational equity. It provides an overview of the elements necessary to create a "systematic, systemic, and sustainable" approach to closing the achievement gap.

Directions: Using the scale below, place a checkmark next to your response to each statement. Each number below represents the following responses:

1 : We haven't considered it.   2 : Discussions have taken place.
3 : Initial action has begun.   4 : We are fully engaged.   5 : Action has been completed.

A.	We are engaged in discussions about what cultural responsiveness and equity would look like.	1	2	3	4	5
B.	The organization is inquiry- and solution-centered versus problem-centered regarding equity.	1	2	3	4	5
C.	We understand our organization's strength and barriers impacting equity success.	1	2	3	4	5
D.	We have established accountabilities to address equity.	1	2	3	4	5
E.	Educational equity strategies are aligned with the organization's vision and mission.	1	2	3	4	5
F.	Cultural responsiveness and equity have been integrated into all organizational communications.	1	2	3	4	5
G.	The curriculum is aligned both horizontally and vertically with a focus on cultural responsiveness.	1	2	3	4	5
H.	Culturally responsive professional development has been provided for all stakeholders.	1	2	3	4	5
I.	Practices are in place to attract, recruit, and retain qualified diverse staff.	1	2	3	4	5
J.	The organization has developed mutually beneficial strategies to foster positive relations with the diverse communities it serves.	1	2	3	4	5
K.	Administrators, staff, and faculty are held accountable in their performance reviews to cultural responsiveness and equity objectives.	1	2	3	4	5
L.	Equity improvement strategies are regularly reviewed and reported to all stakeholders.	1	2	3	4	5

REVIEW THE RESULTS

Now that you've worked through the two assessments, where do you see opportunities to enhance (or begin) the Educational Equity Journey? If you are just beginning, don't fret, this book has tools to help you get there.

4 HOW AN ORGANIZATIONAL DEVELOPMENT (OD) EFFORT HELPED ACHIEVE EQUITY

Introduction

We begin this chapter with a review of the challenges facing Dr. Harper when he made the decision to seek outside expertise to guide his efforts to achieve educational equity. Rapid growth had elicited many concerns from long-time White residents fearful that the influx of Hispanic and African American students would lower the quality of the schools. But the new racial and demographic changes required people to look at their assumptions.

Dr. Harper had heard one of his administrators comment about the growing number of students of color: "These kids just haven't yet had time to acclimate to our higher expectations." Mike Kelly, board president, said: "We are at a crossroads. Some White community members want to blame these kids for being here, but it wasn't their fault. They are just here."

Dr. Harper recalled painful staff conversations about racial stereotypes and marginalization.

He realized the district's leadership, while well intentioned, did not have the skill sets to address how issues of race and multiculturalism impacted community relations and student performance. He knew he needed help. During this time, he learned about Bea Young and her unique approach to helping school districts achieve equity success, an approach called the Educational Equity Journey.

Organizational Development Background and Approach

To understand Bea Young's work, it is helpful to consider some background. German American psychologist Kurt Lewin[8] (1890–1947) was among the first to study group dynamics and their application to organizations. His students went on to found the National Training Lab (NTL) in Bethel, ME, where group-based organizational development (OD) consulting practices originated.[9] In the 1950s, they coined the term "organizational development" to define an innovative change effort that fit no traditional consulting category known at the time.

OD interventions focus on identifying the current state of an organization including the clarity of its mission, long-term vision, and actual versus stated core values. This approach is concerned with helping the organization identify the forces that are defining its current state and what needs to be done to achieve its ideal state. OD is most concerned with the seldom-addressed cultural realities that are keeping the organization and its members from achieving their true potential. The process concentrates on building the capacity of the people in the organization to diagnose their current situation, get a commitment to a vision of long-term success and the action steps necessary to begin and sustain the change process.

> To the degree that people are clear about an organization's purpose and there is support and agreement about how to achieve the goals, the organization is effective.

Most OD initiatives, like the Educational Equity Journey, begin when key decision-makers realize the institution has or anticipates a problem and values the input of all individuals and groups. At its core, it makes

---

8   Kurt Lewin, "Frontiers of Group Dynamics: Concept, Method and Reality in Social Science, Social Equilibria, and Social Change," *Human Relations*, 1 (1947): 5–41.

9   Art Kleiner, *The Age of Heretics: Heroes, Outlaws and the Forerunners of Corporate Change* (New York: Doubleday, 1996), pp. 27–60.

the assumption that people work for their own best interests within the context of their organization. If there is clarity about an organization's purpose and support and agreement about how to achieve the goals, the organization can be effective. The assessment and feedback process is the mechanism through which leaders can identify whether structures, relationships, and rewards are either in alignment or out of sync with the understanding of those within the organization. In that sense, OD interventions are both bottom-up and top-down. The motivation to change is strongly related to action. If people are included in making decisions impacting them, they are more likely to adopt the changes.

Bea Young's Experience with Organizational Development

Bea Young's earliest experiences with OD began when she was the education director and then the executive director of the Illinois Commission on Human Relations from 1965 through 1974.

Utilizing OD strategies learned at NTL, Young's team was recognized as one of the state's most effective agencies for their focus on providing support to Illinois cities outside of Chicago that were racially integrating their schools and communities.

After leaving the commission, she gained further experience with prominent OD practitioners/professors within her University of Chicago doctoral program, followed by an OD postgraduate program at the Gestalt Institute of Cleveland, OH. From the late '70s through the early '90s, Young was the principal of Managing Change, the Chicago Division of Harbridge House, Inc., a major international consulting firm. Managing scores of corporate clients during these twenty years, Young honed her skills as an OD practitioner. In 1993, this work continued when she founded the Kaleidoscope Group in Chicago, which focused on workplace diversity and inclusion issues. In 2010, she began to refocus her vision from the corporate world to educational organizations. Her colleagues recall her adamantly saying, "It's time to stop patching up the mistakes of the past in corporations and focus on educational organizations. Here, there's an opportunity to prevent the wrongs of racism before they become baked in. No child is born a racist; it's something that's learned; we can unlearn it in young people."

With that focus, Young developed a new OD model, devised to meet the unique needs of educational organizations, called the "Educational Equity Journey." It was this particular OD practice that became what Dr. Ayala called "the plate upon which the success of everything rests."

What sets OD apart from many other consulting practices? It provides a way to find solutions from within the organization, rather than imposing external knowledge based on the consultant's expertise or other organizations' best practices. As described in the success stories in chapters 1 and 2, the OD efforts engaged a cross-section of the organization in a process that was self-reflective and respectful of all the experiences and knowledge present within each school district.

> No child is born a racist; it's something that's learned. We can unlearn it in young people.

Cultural audits and feedback were critical elements of these OD efforts. Managing the needed change for the districts was based upon actionable suggestions that came through stakeholders' feedback, hence, the term "action research."

The Educational Equity Journey Model at Plainfield District 202

"Our work is driven by the three S's: Systematic, Systemic, and Sustainable," affirm Dr. Ayala and Bea Young. Within the context of a school district, Young defines systemic as "examining the entire educational system in terms of how all parts interrelate, not just looking at isolated parts." While an achievement gap or discussions about race may seem like issues to tackle individually, educational equity can best be addressed by a systemic approach.

Bea Young was engaged in 2005 by District 202 principally for her firm's recognized expertise in racial diversity issues. However, by contracting with the firm, Dr. Harper received an added benefit: Young's career was grounded in OD.

Educational Equity Journey

Cultural Audit
Internal: School Districts and Universities
External: Parents and Community

Audit
Report
Anonymous
Feedback

Measurement
and
Accountability

Leadership
Commitment
to
Educational
Equity

Integrate
Learning
with
Systems

Implementation
Systems and
Initiatives

Cultural
Responsiveness
Education

© 2018 Bea Young Associates, LLC

We can learn more about how this model works by looking at illustrations of each component of the Journey with examples from School District 202:

- **Leadership Commitment to Educational Equity** is the nucleus around which success revolves.

    Before beginning his work with Bea, Dr. Harper already knew his leadership did not have a unified vision for what educational equity meant at District 202. He had a personal commitment to create an equitable environment for all the district's students, but he knew his efforts could not succeed unless he created an organizational commitment. It began with him, and he knew it would take a major effort to get the attention of his entire staff. Consequently, Bea set the stage through an initial professional development effort focusing on diversity and inclusion. This effort involved all twenty-four hundred employees, leaders, administrators, teaching and support staff. With that introductory effort accomplished, Dr. Harper and Bea turned to the first step on the journey, the cultural audits, which she knew would help create leadership alignment with Dr. Harper's vision.

- The **cultural audit** is a process of conducting anonymous and confidential individual interviews with board members, senior staff, and homogeneous focus groups of administrators, teachers, support staff, students, parents, and community leaders. The goal of the cultural audit is to determine how an organization's values and ideals show up (or not) in performance, and to help offer actionable ideas as needed.

Leaders, administrators, teachers, support staff, and students are the core stakeholders of the school system. For these groups, the process is called an **internal audit**. It reveals "connects and disconnects" between stated values and how they're realized within the district's policies, procedures, and curriculum. Where there is a "connect" or an agreement around stated goals and institutional practice, the cultural audit reveals an "organizational strength." Where there is a "disconnect" for any constituency between stated goals and practice, the process reveals an "opportunity for improvement." Regardless of whether the information gathered is a "connect" or "disconnect," it becomes actionable. For example, two summary cultural audit findings illustrating disconnects at District 202 read as follows:

> *"Communication is perceived as one-way by Blacks, humiliating, at times, by Latinos, while perceived with decidedly high marks by Whites."*

> *"Black and Latino students perceive double standards regarding discipline, from doing 'nothing at all' to 'overreacting,' while White students' racially charged behaviors occurred with authorities not taking a stand."*

When engaging the larger community within the school district, the process is called an **external audit**. Like an internal audit, it reveals "connects" and "disconnects" between the district's stated vision and how school policies impact parents, political and institutional leaders, and the community. The "connects" frequently reveal innovative ways to access existing resources. "Disconnects," called "opportunities for improvement," reveal needs either in the district or within the community. Again, the aim is to gather actionable information. Examples from District 202 revealed parents grappling with two issues, as seen from different perspectives:

> *"Some White parents fear the academic bar has been lowered, while Latino parents see their children are not being challenged."*

> *"Black and Latino parents viewed the absence of role models of color as lessening their children's chances of success, while some White parents viewed the conscious pursuit of such role models as 'special treatment' for others."*

In our increasingly diverse school systems, homogeneous focus groups are required, and they must be led by outside facilitators of similar race or ethnic or religious groups to create the trust and openness needed to capture the diverse perceptions of the current culture and practices. The questions, approved in advance by the superintendent, assess the effectiveness of existing initiatives, practices, and strategies to see how they are, or can be, more effectively linked to diversity and equity.

- **The Audit Report of Anonymous Feedback** is the next step.

 The anonymous feedback report was first presented to the superintendent and the board of education and structured around both strengths and opportunities for improvement regarding each key theme.

 Dr. Harper presented the findings and quotes from the cultural audits to all district leaders. He then went a step further and asked his cabinet to read the findings and quotes out loud. The comments were painful to hear. But Bea recalled that, unlike the "tears of despair" during the leadership commitment stage, these were "tears of awareness."

 Through this anonymous feedback process, District 202's leadership began to understand the difference between equality and equity in education. They took on the task of looking inward to become aware of their own cultural lens, while more keenly appreciating the diversity of their schools and communities. They became committed to seeing the educational equity journey as a way of supporting the efforts guided by Dr. Ayala, then assistant superintendent.

- **Integrate Learning with Systems** is the next stage of the model.

  Summarizing the ideas coming from the cultural audits, BYA created a planning matrix identifying five major themes. The board and district administration agreed to act in accordance with the themes. Each theme included proposed action items and accompanying timelines to make it actionable. The document also proudly displayed the new District Equity Action Team purpose statement: "We are committed to closing the achievement gap by embracing the impact of social, emotional, linguistic, and cultural diversity on student learning in an inclusive educational environment."

  One example of the themes identified was a "Lack of diverse representation throughout the district." Three of the five action items associated with this theme included: (1) spread the recruiting net wider; (2) create a diverse selection interview committee; and (3) hold directors accountable to increase recruitment of staff of color.

  Another of the themes identified was the "Need for consistent, two-way communication." Two related action items were (1) "create a parent/community website devoted to diversity and equity at District 202" and (2) "create a District Equity Action Team, including representatives of each stakeholder group."

  This is the stage where the Educational Equity Journey addresses the systemic issues within an organization. What is learned from the cultural audits is different in every school district. Consequently, there is no formula that can predict what needs to be changed. Identifying the themes and action items based on the audits allows each district to create their own customized roadmap for closing the achievement gap.

- **Cultural Responsiveness Education** implements appropriate professional development based on the organizational needs identified by the cultural audits. The ability to evaluate success and organizational impact is a critical outcome of any training or professional development.

  An example of this at District 202 was the professional development facilitated for the newly formed District Equity Action Team.

To keep the focus on the cultural responsiveness to be incorporated into the curriculum, Bea introduced her senior associate and expert in cultural responsiveness curriculum, Susan O'Halloran, to the district. In collaboration with Dr. Ayala, Sue conducted workshops to help SAC members infuse cultural responsiveness into the curriculum, as described in chapter 6. Cultural responsiveness education will be different for every school district based on needs and opportunities identified in the cultural audits.

- **Implementation of Systems and Initiatives** builds inclusive action steps and communication strategies. Building on the previous steps, this process ensures the organization is moving forward to implement what they have learned.

  District 202 accomplished this stage through assigning clear equity goals within their five-year plan.

  Since the need for effective two-way communication had been identified as a key audit theme, Dr. Harper chose to create the position of director of community relations. Ably handled by Tom Hernandez, this position was key to the district's internal communications and external public relations. Tom saw an opportunity to spread the word about the extraordinary gains at Plainfield District 202, especially regarding English language learners. Creating a position to communicate the district's progress in closing the achievement gap and improving community relations was a critical part of the district's implementation plan.

> The educational equity journey is not a "quick fix." It's a journey!

- **Measurement and Accountability** is the final phase of the educational equity journey. It ensures that accountability for each part of the implementation plan is assigned and progress is measured. Assigning accountability is key to any action completion, whether it's a long-term plan or a list of short-term activities. Adding equity accountability in each leader's performance review was a key component of measurement.

Measuring results completes the cycle by providing feedback that allows school leaders to determine what's working and what may need to be done differently.

The Educational Equity Journey is not a "quick fix." It's a journey! The key is to use both formal and informal measurements to recognize whether the actions within the district align with its stated vision of educational equity. Some school districts have implemented a second cultural audit after about two to five years to ascertain what changes have been sustained and where new issues may have emerged.

5 MOVING FROM EXCLUSION TO INCLUSIVE BEHAVIORS

In February 2018, Dr. Ayala received the following email from one of her middle school students:

"I am an eighth grade student at Lincoln Middle School here in the Berwyn area. I stand on behalf of the African American culture/ community in Berwyn. I feel that this community, which is mostly Hispanic, does not give light on the African American community. As a Black man myself, I am offended. Why is it that other cultures are embraced in the schools and community events, yet one culture that plays the most essential role in American history is not celebrated nor is embarked on?

The last time I learned about my culture's history in Berwyn was in fifth grade. Why stop there? I emailed my school principal on this same matter and said, 'I had a thought going through my head for quite some time now, and it was the thought of why our school doesn't celebrate Black history. I feel that my race's background is not established to the extent it should be here at LMS. I feel our history should be incorporated greatly in social studies and ELA. Our race's history is important in society today, and kids today only learn the small pieces to the history of African Americans.'

Why should that stop once they get in middle school? Why not keep it going? There is more to Black history than MLK or Rosa Parks. People like Claudette Colvin, Malcolm X, Harold Washington, the Black Panthers, Nat Turner, Booker T. Washington, Mansa Musa, etc., all should be studied in depth in middle school.

My principal has yet to respond, but she has seen the email. She had a meeting with the social studies teachers about my email, and it opened up not only her eyes but the social studies teachers as well. My social studies teacher said it is 'sad' that we

*don't talk about it. I know it has to do with curriculum, but it
[also] has to do with the voices in the community. I am proud to
be Black because 'Black is beautiful.' I carry so much history on
my shoulders that stems from African American struggles. Yet my
culture is put on the backhand. What does that mean? It means
that my culture is not talked about here in the community.*

*Dr. Ayala, there is an argument to be made here in Berwyn
and that is the need of the African American culture. The rich soil,
which is nurtured by African Americans. Read my argument and
understand it deeply. Take action on this plan. I would also like to
meet with you if that is fine to talk more about this matter."*

"I couldn't have been prouder of this student," asserts Dr. Ayala. "It
demonstrated we created an environment we hoped for when we began
the inclusive behaviors workshops for principals in 2015. Reinforced by
teacher professional development, posters in hallways, and even performance
evaluations, it was clear at least one student knew it was okay to
take a stand on a curriculum issue about which he felt strongly and take
it to the boss without fear. But I was uncomfortable, too. My discomfort
resonated with his discomfort. How would the staff receive this feedback?
How would the board receive this?"

Dr. Ayala met with this student—let's call him Douglass—and three
others shortly after receiving his email. It resulted in two of the students
standing before the certified teachers during a Teacher Institute and before
the board of education during one of their regular meetings. The
students created a PowerPoint and very respectfully, eloquently, and passionately
made their voices heard.

> When we view education from an inclusive perspective, we must ask ourselves, "Who is not at the table?

"In the end, there was an incredible sense of pride. Douglass was one
of two students given the superintendent's award for exemplifying personal, academic, and civic potential,
the three pillars in Berwyn North's mission philosophy statement, during
that year's promotion ceremony. The message these students needed to

deliver was received, respected, and acted upon. This was a reminder that equity is a journey, and we need to use these opportunities to continue to elevate the importance of cultural responsiveness throughout the district. I wondered what the reaction might have been had District 98 not embarked upon the educational equity journey and the inclusive behaviors training?"

How often do we hear our students express their passion about their culture? Douglass "took a stand" for his community and his education. How can we create a learning community positioned to receive this type of feedback from our students?

Encouraging Inclusive Behaviors: A Critical Component of Creating Cultural Responsiveness

The story above illustrates one of many instances at District 98 where staff were challenged to look through a lens other than their own. When we are striving for educational equity, the lens we use shifts our worldview to include what's seen through our students' eyes. How often have we not recognized our students' cultural concerns? When we view education from an inclusive perspective, we must ask ourselves, "Who is not at the table? Whose perspectives are missing? Do we have the skills to hear them? Are we addressing the needs of all our students?"

Learning how to hear different perspectives does not come naturally. Instead, it's common to become defensive or go into attack mode. Doing either is a sure way of shutting down communication. Without open, honest communication, learning doesn't occur. At the root of how this learning occurs is something we call inclusion and exclusion.

Inclusive versus Exclusive Behaviors Model

The inclusive and exclusive behaviors model developed by coauthor Bea Young was introduced at District 202's institute days and staff orientations during Dr. Ayala's tenure there. After Dr. Ayala became District 98 superintendent and having seen how integral this training was in creating a culturally responsive environment in her previous position, she provided professional development for all staff in inclusive behaviors training. She understood that learning, practicing, and utilizing the inclusive behaviors on a day-to-day basis can be a key component for diminishing the gap in achievement between students of color and White students.

Inclusive vs Exclusive Behaviors

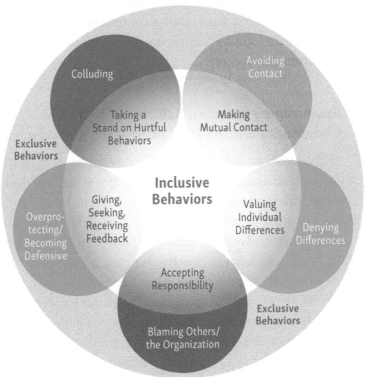

© 2018 Bea Young Associates, LLC

Unconsciously, both insiders and outsiders engage in the five exclusive behaviors we call "avoiding contact," "denying differences," "blaming others," "becoming defensive or overprotective," and "colluding." Unfortunately, people often engage in exclusive behaviors because they prefer what is most comfortable or most familiar. But it is often these exclusive behaviors that create the inability to work together or see situations from another perspective.

Exclusive behaviors can be unlearned. For every exclusive behavior, there's an inclusive behavior to counteract it. Making mutual contact can replace avoiding contact. Valuing differences is the opposite of denying differences. Accepting responsibility overcomes blaming others. Giving, seeking, and receiving feedback, while difficult, are always better alternatives than overprotection or defensiveness. And taking a stand—sometimes the most difficult of all—is better than living the misunderstandings implicit in collusion.

Learning the inclusive behaviors in a way that applies to your school organization is straightforward but not easy. The first rule is "become comfortable with discomfort."

Having introduced the model, let's return to the story about Douglass to see what inclusive behaviors he demonstrated. Despite the clear discomfort about the issue, Douglass demonstrated all the inclusive behaviors, first in his email and later in actions:

> Exclusive behaviors can be unlearned.

- *Making Mutual Contact:* Douglass identified and reached out to all the individuals who he believed could help him achieve his goal. He persisted when he felt he wasn't being heard, and he asked for discussion and mutual conversation.
- *Valuing Individual Differences:* Both Douglass and Dr. Ayala were aware they were coming from very different positions of power, education, age, gender, and ethnic identity within the district. In many cases, any one of those differences would be enough to stop the conversation. Even though she, too, was uncomfortable with the issue he was bringing up, Dr. Ayala saw in his email a young man using every inclusive behavior he could muster. His issues were real, and she knew he needed to be heard. Douglass was asking for the inclusion of Black history as a part of American history. Crucially, he stated that the history "should be incorporated," suggesting his idea would benefit other students. By requesting the history be included rather than be part of replacing other elements taught in history, Douglass showed respect for the other histories currently being taught and respect for his fellow students.
- *Accepting Responsibility:* Douglass was very clear that his concern about

the absence of Black studies in the curriculum was both a community and personal issue for him. He owned his feelings and did not attempt to blame the organization or the social studies teachers.

- *Giving, Seeking, and Receiving Feedback:* Douglass provided specific names and information about other historical figures he believed should be included in a middle school curriculum. He also sought out Dr. Ayala for ideas about how he could make the change. She coached him on how to create an effective PowerPoint presentation to make his case to staff and board of education members. A comment by one of the social studies teachers who called his situation "sad" is an example of an exclusive behavior; a well-intended sympathetic, but overprotective, remark, which for most students might have stopped the effort.
- *Taking a Stand:* Ultimately, this story is about taking a stand. It would have been easy for Douglass to go along and accept that he couldn't change the curriculum. He knew both he and other members of the African American community felt their issues were, as he said, "put on the backhand." He was willing to keep working until he at least felt heard.

One student using these inclusive behaviors was able to make a profound change in his school. How much more of an impact is possible when the leaders of a school or school district apply inclusive behaviors with the same respectful determination as Douglass?

While simple in concept, using the inclusive behaviors requires a school system to support these tools visibly and practically through its policies. They require professional development and training on how to become conscious of using the inclusive behaviors. This also involves developing an awareness of our unconscious and unintentional use of the exclusive behaviors and their negative impacts on others. Most importantly, they require administrators, teachers, staff, and students alike to develop a level of comfort with what is almost always uncomfortable—talking about differences, especially those involving race and culture, which, because of our history, drive to our deepest fears. But if Douglass, an eighth grader, can do it . . .

Impacts of Inclusive Behaviors Training at District 98

The organization that Dr. Ayala inherited in 2012 was healthy in many respects. Yet, when viewed through the perspective of how responsive the District was to the needs of its students and the Berwyn North community, there were a number of concerns that failed the litmus test of inclusion. Looking through the lens of our exclusive behaviors, Dr. Ayala encountered:

- *Avoiding Contact:* Though 82 percent of the school population was Hispanic, the district was disconnected from the Hispanic community. Minimal information was provided in Spanish. Staffing in the district was not reflective of the student population. Parents were turned away rather than included in the conversation if they did not speak English. Many Hispanic parents felt unwelcome or unable to participate fully in parent-teacher conferences.
- *Denying Differences:* The curriculum was outdated and did not truly reflect the district's diverse community. Incidents of support staff feeling treated as "less than" were reported often.
- *Blaming Others:* It was common to hear staff talk about the lack of family involvement and blame the parents for students' poor achievement.
- *Defensiveness:* Teachers felt judged for not having Spanish-speaking skills. Some teachers and parents felt that changes were being made that would not benefit them.
- *Colluding:* Community members were uncomfortable sharing concerns and held back sharing with school officials. The board of education was receiving many anonymous complaints with no way of ascertaining veracity or following up on possible concerns.

After completing both internal and external cultural audits at District 98 in 2013, three recommendations emerged that launched the work around the inclusive behaviors:

1. **Create Inclusive Behaviors Professional Development** for all administrators and district specialists. The unique aspect of this training was a "train-the-trainer" approach, which made these individuals responsible for providing the same behavior skill-building throughout

the rest of the organization, including teaching and support staff. Their role was not only to train but to model and reinforce the inclusive behaviors throughout the district.

2. **Create Collaborative Community and School Cultural Responsiveness Training.** To help build bridges between the district and the community a core group—including teachers, parents, and community leaders—was created to inform the instructional five-year plan.

3. **Offer Instructional Cultural Responsiveness Training** for the SACs. This was instituted to help build cultural responsiveness throughout all subject areas.

By 2014 the board of education had approved a district instructional five-year plan, which incorporated these three recommendations to create an environment in which educational equity could thrive. And by 2015 the inclusive behaviors professional development modules were first rolled out. This work is ongoing.

District 98 has already experienced a number of key changes when viewed through the lens of inclusion. At an Illinois Association of School Administrators (IASA) conference in 2018, Dr. Ayala could report the following changes:

- *Making Mutual Contact:* Forms, marquees, district and school newsletters, and messages were available in both English and Spanish. The district had increased community outreach through events more reflective of the community. Hiring of Black and Hispanic staff at teaching and administration levels better reflects the demographics of the community.

- *Valuing Individual Differences:* There now exists a rigorous curriculum with multicultural content included throughout. Representation from the entire community is now part of the process when choosing membership in key committees and meetings.

- *Accepting Responsibility:* Informal staff and community dialogue is now encouraged through community coffee meetups. The inclusive behaviors have become part of the way staff hold each other accountable.

- *Giving, Seeking, and Receiving Feedback:* District Staff now ask the question "Who's not at the table?" when considering membership and participation in any organizational change effort.

- *Taking a Stand:* The board of education and administration no longer respond to anonymous letters. The community coffees have become a safe place for parents to provide critical feedback to the organization. The district is viewed as becoming more welcoming to all parent and community voices.

Taking It to Your Districts and Schools

It's our experience that, as you employ the inclusive behaviors within your respective organizations, you will become more effective as administrators, teachers, or team members. You will also enhance interactions you have with students and staff entrusted to you. As demonstrated in the organizational changes beginning to be reported at District 98, using inclusive behaviors is about more than building personal communication skills. These behaviors are also building blocks, which can help refocus a school organization on its equity mission by creating the structures, systems, and philosophy that support all stakeholders in the organization.

> Children have extraordinary antennae for picking up what's being said through our actions.

The inclusive behaviors model we have used on the educational equity journey doesn't require you to change beliefs or values. However, it does require you to pay attention to those around you. Behaviors have consequences. Children have extraordinary antennae for picking up what's being said through our actions. And, as adults, we carry an inner child aware of subtle slights, outright hurts, or unconscious misunderstandings, and this inner child impacts our ability to work well together.

The Urgency of Now: Inclusive and Culturally Responsive Schools

To further implement inclusive behaviors, we also have to look into the classrooms and at the relationships that affect students most directly. Roughly 80 percent of our teachers are young, White women, who intend the best for their students. Often, they have been given little to no training about how to reach and teach children of diverse backgrounds. Nationally, there is a disturbing trend showing the lack of connection that continues to grow between White teachers and students of color.[10] Thus, even when teachers are armed with good intentions, it is important that they are also prepared to address the issues of insiders and outsiders within their classrooms.

In a recent article entitled "10 Ways Well-Meaning White Teachers Bring Racism into Our Schools," Jamie Utt emphasizes how we lower or raise achievement expectations based on race and ethnicity and whether the teacher perceives her student as an outsider. Similarly, Utt describes how discipline practices disproportionately impact students of color. That is, young Black males (outsiders) are viewed as combative, while White males (insiders) are viewed as achievers. According to Utt, "In virtually every school in the country, from the most mono-racial to the most diverse, discipline practices are set up to fail students of color . . . there are dire consequences for students who 'struggle with discipline problems' in our world of hyper-criminalization."[11]

A 2014 study published in the *New York Times* concludes that "[m]any of the nation's largest districts had very different disciplinary rates for students of different races . . . [F]or example . . . in Chicago, they [Black students] made up 45 percent of the students, but 76 percent of the suspensions."[12] To address this issue, Illinois signed into law August 2015 Senate Bill 100 requiring all public schools to address their disproportionate disciplinary practices.

The damage to each individual life brought about by failing discipline practices within schools is often insurmountable. These practices have long-lasting consequences, frequently taking a student from the classroom to lockup. That consideration needs to be paramount.

---

10 Motoko Rich, "Where Are the Teachers of Color?" *New York Times*, April 11, 2015, https://www.nytimes.com/2015/04/12/sunday-review/where-are-the-teachers-of-color.html.

11 Jamie Utt, "10 Ways Well-Meaning White Teachers Bring Racism into Our Schools," *Everyday Feminism*, August 26, 2015, https://everydayfeminism.com/2015/08/10-ways-well-meaning-white-teachers-bring-racism-into-our-schools/.

12 Leah Sakala, *Breaking Down Mass Incarceration in the 2010 Census: State-by-State Incarceration Rates by Race/Ethnicity* (Prison Policy Initiative, May 28, 2014), https://www.prisonpolicy.org/reports/rates.html.

And, from a public perspective, not only is it humanly indefensible, but it's costly: "Before spending a single dollar on education, mental health care, or substance abuse treatment for youth in prison, Illinois annually devotes $187,765 per youth to operate its five youth prisons."[13] In contrast, Illinois spends only $8,024 per student to fund public K–12 education (2018 Illinois State Report Card instructional amount per student).

The famous African American historian, Dr. W. E. B. Du Bois, who in 1895 became the first Black man to receive his PhD from Harvard University, said in his seminal 1903 book *The Souls of Black Folk*, "The problem of the Twentieth Century will be the problem of the color-line."[14] And so it remains in this, the twenty-first century.

Closing the achievement gap first documented in the 1966 Coleman Report is not only part of an indictment as predicted by Dr. Du Bois, but is a national tragedy writ large with implications for the country's ability to compete in the world economy. A 2009 report by McKinsey and Company asserts that the persistence of the achievement gap in the US has the economic effect of a "permanent national recession."[15] But, more importantly, this failure of the schools is played out daily in the lives of many individual children of color who might as well be living in a third-world country. Changing the achievement gap is at the core of each school's effort to achieve educational equity.

The systemic use of the five inclusive behaviors for staff professional development, as implemented first at Plainfield District 202 and in Berwyn North District 98, demonstrates that students of color can close the achievement gap when teachers and school systems change their approach. Significantly, as reported in chapter 1, not only did students of color overcome the achievement gap, but White children excelled beyond expectations as well. Further, similar results are already being achieved in District 98. It becomes a win-win for all.

---

13 Stephanie Kollmann, "The Costliest Choice: Economic Impact of Youth Incarceration," *Community Safety and the Future of Illinois' Youth Prisons*, vol. 3, March 2018, https://docplayer .net/79486766-The-costliest-choice-economic-impact-of-youth-incarceration.html.

14 W. E. B. Du Bois, *The Souls of Black Folk* (Chicago: A. C. McClurg & Co., 1903), p. 1.

15 *The Economic Impact of the Achievement Gap in America's Schools* (McKinsey & Company, April 2009), https://dropoutprevention.org/wp-content/uploads/2015/07/ACHIEVEMENT_GAP_ REPORT_20090512.pdf.

Insights into the Frequency of Your Inclusive Behaviors

Now, take a deep breath. You have been given a lot of information, concepts, and actual experiences to consider. You may already have ideas about where you want to start in making a difference. Maybe you have been taking notes in the margins. If you're wondering how to implement what you have learned so far, consider starting here. Take a measure of yourself by responding to the following inclusive behaviors self-assessment checklist.

FIVE INCLUSIVE BEHAVIORS CHECKLIST

Based on the rating scales below, mark the numbers in the spaces to the right to indicate how often you engage in each behavior.

1 : Hardly Ever   2 : Not Often   3 : Sometimes   4 : Often   5 : Very Often

To what extent do I . . .

MAKING MUTUAL CONTACT	FREQUENCY
Share my knowledge and experiences with people from different backgrounds	
Encourage involvement of racially and culturally diverse community groups	
Support activities that enable students from diverse cultural groups to work together	
Provide support or mentoring to racially and culturally diverse colleagues	

VALUING INDIVIDUAL DIFFERENCES	FREQUENCY
Ask "Who is not at the table?" when key decisions are being made	
Respect and encourage styles and approaches that are different than my own	
Publicly acknowledge that cultural responsiveness is how we create greater success	
Take time to learn about different cultures and communities in my area	

ACCEPTING RESPONSIBILITY	FREQUENCY
Sincerely apologize for the negative impact of any of my actions and clarify my intentions	
Acknowledge my biases and assumptions and work to challenge them	
Model the behaviors I expect from others	
Help those with whom I work to believe they can make a difference	

GIVING, SEEKING, AND RECEIVING FEEDBACK	FREQUENCY
Give constructive, non-judgmental feedback to help others learn and grow	
Uncover concerns people have with me, asking, "How well are we working together?"	
Listen to others' feedback with an open mind	
Compliment others' inclusive behaviors	

TAKING A STAND ON HURTFUL BEHAVIORS	FREQUENCY
Respectfully challenge behaviors or messages that can create exclusion	
Ask others to alert me if I'm unconsciously treating someone unfairly	
Encourage discussion of cultural bias and its impact on individuals	
Implement practices and demonstrate behaviors that support cultural responsiveness	

TO ASSESS YOUR RESULTS:

1. Look for areas where you rated yourself with scores of 1 or 2; these are "opportunities for improvement." We challenge you to take action.

2. If you rated yourself with mostly 3s, you are on the path to equity; keep moving.

3. If you have scores of 4 or 5, we celebrate you and know you will bring others to the educational equity journey.

6 COMPONENTS OF A CULTURALLY RESPONSIVE CURRICULUM

A junior-year history class was given the assignment of writing about one of the founding fathers of this country. An African American high school student had just about had it with studying and writing about "these White dudes who owned slaves." He asked his teacher if he might instead write about the Black Panthers.

The teacher replied, "No. This is history class. I don't want you writing about some sports team."

The student banged his desk and kicked it in absolute frustration.

In the teacher's defense, she hadn't even been alive when the Black Panthers were tutoring, running medical clinics, and working as revolutionary activists in the 1960s. African American history, issues, and contributions had not been a part of her education.

But how wonderful if she had paused for just a moment and said, "Tell me more about the Black Panthers and why you want to write about them."

—by Susan O'Halloran, Senior Associate at BYA and Nationally Acclaimed Storyteller

The student's response of kicking the desk was a behavior that needed to be addressed. However, his feelings were understandable. Day after day, year after year, that young man spent a large part of his day in a school or, in this particular case, a class that didn't acknowledge him or his community's history.

This is an illustration of the importance of educators getting to know their students and understanding their own mis-education, blind spots, and racial conditioning. If we have students from cultures about which we are unfamiliar, as educators we need to ask ourselves, "What don't I know? Who can I ask? Where can I get more information about this group's history, popular culture, and the people from this culture whom my students admire?"

The culturally responsive curriculum model can offer insights to help educators develop curriculum:

Components of Culturally Responsive Curriculum

CORE CURRICULUM—Is curriculum content developed by subject matter experts convened throughout the district? Is the curriculum aligned horizontally and vertically for each grade level within the district?

INDIVIDUAL—Are resources and time provided for educators to learn about individual students and how they learn?

FAMILY AND COMMUNITY—Is subject matter reflective of students' home cultures? Are educators encouraged to reflect on their own cultural lens to look at subject matter differently?

SOCIETY—Does the subject matter show you care about the world in which your students live and empower them to be active members of society?

Whenever a student can say "YES! This subject is about me, my family, and my world," that's the aim of a culturally responsive curriculum.

© 2017 Susan O'Halloran

CORE CURRICULUM is the subject matter content for which educators are responsible and students will be expected to learn. When subject matter experts create curriculum that is vertically and horizontally aligned, as in Districts 202 and 98, students are prepared to engage in the next three components.

INDIVIDUAL refers to making lessons responsive to individual students (i.e., creating subject matter that relates to an individual student's interests, hobbies, and personal styles). Students are always part of and separate from their home cultures. Two students from the same ethnic background, for example, may have very different values, ideas, and ways of expressing their identity and culture. While the student at the start of this chapter had an interest in the Black Panthers, it does not mean that other students with similar backgrounds in the same city and school would have similar interests. Paying attention to how each student is unique is key to respecting the great diversity within each cultural group.

FAMILY and COMMUNITY creates ways for the students to see reflections of their families and their home cultures in your school. Part of showing respect for children is to recognize and relate to what they already know and bring to the classroom. We recognize that their home cultures fulfill our students' deep psychological need for a strong sense of self and historical continuity.

SOCIETY acknowledges the larger world in which the students live. Science, math, and any other subject aren't only strict transfers of knowledge about proven theories and principles. They happen in a world of hierarchies and harmonies, of empowerment and power imbalances; no subject exists in a vacuum.

When the core curriculum (red) intersects with the unique interests and strengths of individual students (light green) plus the students' home cultures (blue) and the economic and sociopolitical worlds in which students live (dark green), then we've hit the target (center) of becoming relevant and culturally responsive to our students. Of course, we can't spend all our teaching time in the target area where these four components overlap, but the more we do, the better chance we have of engaging our students. When we aim for this inclusive target, we are doing our best to make sure no student feels invisible or considers anyone else as "less than." Students who feel welcomed and feel they belong have the greatest possibility of learning as well as behaving inclusively toward others.

Addressing "Blind Spots" through a Culturally Responsive Curriculum

"Welcome to professional development day. I'd like to introduce Susan O'Halloran of Bea Young Associates."

As I heard my name, I walked up to the front of the room. I had been asked to work with District 202 as they were doing the challenging and important work of aligning their curriculum. It began with a professional development day for all the staff who were part of the various subject area committees (SACs). My role was to introduce the concept of cultural responsiveness as well as build strategies to weave cultural content into the subjects for which they were already acknowledged experts.

One of the guiding principles of the workshop was to help the educators understand that a key component of a culturally responsive curriculum is to infuse subject matter content with cultural content that sends the message to students: "You belong—this is your school and classroom."

At that day-long work session, all the educators sat at long cafeteria tables in their huge gymnasium. The walls were lined with their work from the previous day: long banners of butcher paper filled with gradated learning objectives. The teachers could easily see how each learning objective in their subject matter built upon the previous ones and then how the learning baton would be handed to the next grade. What was not so easy was how to send inclusive messages to all students within subjects as disparate as math and history.

As we worked through the lists, one table team began the conversation about how to include children with those "you belong here" messages. They shared the story of a middle school teacher who began her year by asking students of color to introduce themselves to their White classmates by talking about their families' cultural backgrounds. The White students, however, did not introduce themselves similarly as if they didn't have a culture. This simple example quickly galvanized the conversation about what it means to welcome students. Opinions varied.

> Students who feel welcomed and feel they belong have the greatest possibility of learning . . .

Similarly, I was alerted to another educator who throughout the year included his few students of color by asking them questions about the history of their racial or ethnic group's history. "What do you want to tell us about slavery?" and even "Tell us what it's like to come from a tribal society."

It would never occur to this educator to ask his White students to describe their families' tribal backgrounds—for example, what it's like to descend from Celtic or Germanic tribes. No. The White students were being approached as Americans, while the students of color were presented as "others." For example, the teacher's request illustrated that she "doesn't know what she doesn't know" about life in Africa.

These educators' intent was inclusion; however, the impact was quite different. It created exclusion.

I was there to help educators explore culturally responsive curriculum. But what do I mean by "culture" and, by extension, "cultural responsiveness"?

Culture can be defined as a shared design for living. A group of people have lived or participated in a similar place, time, or institution for such a long time—sharing food, language, hardships, values, meaning, and other similar experiences—that they have developed any number of spoken and unspoken agreements about "this is how we do things here."

In that sense, any dimension of diversity (gender, religion, education, generations, etc.) can be designated as culture, but, for the sake of this writing, I'm referring to the dimensions we call ethnicity, nationality, or that social construction identified as "race."

In one of the exercises we did that day, the educators imagined a school day from a student's point of view where they did not receive those welcoming messages:

- Imagine you are constantly asked, "Where are you from?" You hear some of the White students who are on sports teams described as "all-American" boys and girls, but you are never portrayed that way.
- Imagine on your mother's side of the family you are part of the Choctaw Nation. At school, you do a unit on American Indians. Your class is instructed to build teepees out of construction paper. Your ancestors lived in houses, never teepees. The students are further instructed to make Indian "costumes": headbands with feathers. You know your relatives don't and never did wear headbands and that these and other Indian stereotypes are basically an invention of the US film industry. Just as you are about to say something, your friend next to you calls, "Hey, Chief!" and starts whooping as he briskly taps the palm of his hand against his lips. You've never seen any of your relatives at the ceremonial powwows you attend make such a gesture.

- Imagine you are a tenth-grade Lebanese American. You notice that your teacher and several of the students use the words "Arabs" and "Muslims" interchangeably. You are an Arab Christian. No one seems to know this kind of Arab—your kind of Arab—exists and that only 10 percent of Muslims are Arabs.

Next, we walked through a "Day in the Life" where students felt their teachers "got" them and school felt exciting and relevant to their lives:

- Imagine students regularly present history reports from other points of view such as the Battle of the Alamo from a Latino perception or the defeat of Custer from the Lakota Sioux and Cheyenne perspectives.
- Imagine, in math class, your teacher uses a variety of names in word problems such as Latisha, Jorge, and Ahmad instead of only European-sounding names such as Mary and John.
- Imagine, in botany class, you study the scientific discoveries made by Japanese Americans in the incarceration camps during World War II—for example, how they discovered ways of irrigating plants in the desert that we still use today.
- Imagine you regularly study the times people of different backgrounds stood up for each other, such as people in Oberlin, Ohio, in 1858 refusing to let someone be taken back into slavery, the Choctaw Indians raising money for the Irish suffering the potato famine, and Irish Americans who fought with Mexicans for their independence.

The educators observed that, by looking at their subject's content through the eyes and feelings of their diverse students, they felt the inspiration to put in the time, research, and collaboration required to create culturally relevant curriculum. In working with educators, I often show a video I made of my colleague—storyteller and former school librarian Anne Shimojima. She says that while growing up in the 1950s and 60s, whenever someone in the family saw a person of Asian descent on TV, they would shout to the rest of the family, "Asian on TV!" and everyone would come running into the living room to see this rare sight.

Anne describes the first time, in her mid-thirties, when she saw two Asian actors on stage. She had the oddest (and most profound) sensation.

"I realized that because they were there [she points to the imagined stage] I was here [she points to herself]. In my seat, I was here. I existed. I never realized until then how absolutely invisible I had felt. When you look out into the popular culture and there's no one who looks like you, it's like looking into the mirror of life and there's no reflection."

Too many of our students feel they need to leave their home cultures at the door when they walk into our schools. Once in our schools, they feel they have journeyed into some kind of parallel universe.

A Latina friend of mine attended a school where no attempt was made to include her ethnic heritage. She told me she felt that going to school each day was like walking onto an alien planet. At school, she knew she would not hear her language or her music or see her family's food on the Basic Food Group chart nor study the accomplishments of her people.

> ... she felt that going to school each day was like walking onto an alien planet.

We can be the greatest educators in the world, but if our students are struggling with feeling that they aren't valued, that they don't belong, the learning we offer may be for naught. In their book *Anti-Bias Education for Young Children and Ourselves*, Louise Derman-Sparks and Julie Olsen Edwards state, "We cannot know all the consequences of cultural discontinuity for students' development. We do know that children thrive when the school program respects and integrates their home languages and cultures into all aspects of the school program."[16]

As educators, we have a responsibility to give our students both mirrors—to see themselves, to feel visible, to know they count—and windows—to come to understand, appreciate, and value others.

This does not mean we ask our students to become representatives for their group(s). When you broaden the social context of your subject content, you will be exploring the realities of your students' lives. If students

---

16   Louise Derman-Sparks and Julie Olsen Edwards, *Anti-Bias Education for Young Children and Ourselves* (NAEYC, 2010), p. 59, https://www.naeyc.org/resources/pubs/books/anti-bias -education.

volunteer to share their personal experiences, that's one thing. However, you would never say to a student, "Tell us what it's like to be . . ."

Building Cultural Responsiveness into the District 98 Curriculum

At District 98, I had a full day to work with each SAC—math, social studies, fine arts, language arts, physical education, and health. We did some preliminary work on the effect of stereotypes and recognizing our blind spots, because cultural responsiveness isn't just about adding cultural references to our subject matter; it is also about understanding our personal cultural lens. For instance, you might ask yourself:

- What did I hear my parents or other family members say about our group and other groups when I was growing up?
- What was I taught about my students' communities—the barriers they've faced and the victories they've won?
- How much exposure did I have to a diversity of ethnicities and nationalities? From what communities did my heroes, friends, family friends, neighbors, service people, and media consumption come?
- How much contact do I have now with the communities of which my students are a part? How can I create true connections in these communities?

Here's something you can count on. If you grew up with any group that was referred to as "them," "those people," or any number of derogatory terms, then you have misinformation and blind spots about that group. We all have biases and ignorance. None of us are guilty because of what we were or were not exposed to growing up. However, we are all responsible to learn as much as we can now, especially to break up and manage any stereotypes about the groups to which our students belong. Sometimes, we mean well, but we learn one or two attributes of a culture and think "now we know" when, in fact, we just wind up re-stereotyping that group, albeit with a few new twists to the small box in which we place them.

Because of the additional time we had at District 98, we were able go deeper into how the history of different racial and ethnic groups have shaped the cultural conflicts we have today. At various times in US history, people who lived here, worked here, and built this country couldn't hold office, be in the military, sign contracts, assemble in groups, practice their religion, enter many professions, or be admitted to many universities. They could be arrested for vagrancy and, with no due process of law, be farmed out to the highest bidder for four months of labor. Also, people who were not citizens could be forced to be sterilized—just to name a few indignities and privations.

In a short period of time, with example after example of how certain groups were barred from the promise of "liberty and justice for all," teachers came to a deeper understanding of how and why some students may view the "dominant" culture, especially school, with mistrust.

We also took some time to view how their subject matter had been used as an arm of subjugation: the scientific experiments in the Tuskegee study; the norm of "proper" English as an indicator of intelligence; the use of religion to justify atrocities; the teaching of only some people's history from the view of the victor; and so on.

Many educators know that some students have a kind of allergy to school and to society as a whole. When aware of the bigotry and discrimination their students' families and communities have faced, educators are less likely to take any student's resistance personally. Those in the training commented that understanding why some students might feel alienated was a wonderful motivator for devising strategies to build connection and trust with their students.

Louise Derman-Sparks and Julie Olsen Edwards note that "Individualizing and adapting your curriculum (and behavior) according to each student's home culture is as essential to healthy development as substituting cream cheese for peanut butter for the child who is allergic to peanuts."[17]

When we create a culturally relevant curriculum, students learn to value themselves while, at the same time, they thrive with confidence and open-mindedness in a world of immense diversity.

---

17 Derman-Sparks and Edwards, *Anti-Bias Education for Young Children and Ourselves*, p. 62.

EPILOGUE

Looking Back and Moving Forward

How the 1960s School Integration Efforts Underscore Today's Push for Educational Equity

"Just give dialogue a chance. Don't send in the armored cars yet, please." I made eye contact as best I could with the state police officer, seeing myself in his dark, reflective glasses.

My throat was sore from pleading, my nerves taut, my heart pounding. Behind the state police officer stood four more local police, armed and heavy with riot gear. I knew the impacts on a country, a state, a city, or a school district caught between Black and White. How many times did I need to shout and scream to be heard? Probably many times over since I knew in my heart and soul the power of mediation, talking, challenging, and listening versus threats.

This was 1967 in Illinois, and there were many holdout high schools where the mayor and local school superintendent stood firmly in their belief that integration "would not work in our town."

We were continually asked, "What can talking do at a time when tensions are so strong after years of segregation, bias, and misunderstandings?" But our team was also armed—armed with love and understanding for all students and their futures.

—a reflection by Bea Young

This is an example of the resistance I was facing with the introduction of the Coleman Report over fifty years ago. I was the education director for the Illinois Commission on Human Relations. My team's role was to assist school administrators whose responsibilities included enforcing court orders and directives from federal agencies. Illinois school districts were among the first in the North to receive these directives, and they sparked demonstrations, civil disobedience, and intense resistance—some violent—by school boards, administrators, teachers, and parents.

In the situation with the Illinois State Police, they did listen to our pleas and supported us while our team met in the high school gym with Black students on one side and White students on the other side. We asked each student to find someone on the opposite side and become partners for this moment. With questioning looks, many deep sighs, and initial reluctance, the students moved slowly across the gym and quietly found a partner of a different race and took a seat. Suddenly, the room looked very different, felt safer, and was quiet while the students awaited our next instructions. And they did what we know students everywhere can do: they got to know each other's goals, dreams (including their families' dreams), and hopes for the future.

> I remember another particularly tense moment of our 1960s school integration experiences. A tall, muscular, and tense school official stood, with his arms outstretched across his high school front door, as our team tried to enter. This created a standoff that seemed to last forever, with crowds screaming at us and waving placards. They were held back by police. It had been weekly front-page news in the local paper. The community knew we were there to bring White and Black students together.
>
> I recall simply taking the official's hand and walking him through the doors. It was then he quietly turned and said, "Can you help us make this work?" I knew we were all in— emotionally, spiritually, intellectually, and physically—to make his school a better, more peaceful, safer learning space for all. In no small measure, we impacted the desegregation of many Illinois public schools.

This work was highlighted in *Chicago Magazine* in the summer of 1968. The article opened with the following statement from a school administrator, on fire with a new racial sensitivity:

"If not broken, the rose-colored glasses, worn by many of those administrators and teachers in racially troubled schools throughout Illinois, have been smudged. And they've been smudged because of new knowledge, confrontation, a little honest feeling, and, hopefully, more than a little sensitivity to knowing what it's like to be any color other than white at this particular time.

Its goals are deceptively simple—to sensitize school educators to the needs of minority group students, to break down communication barriers, and to initiate badly needed curriculum changes. But, while its goals are seemingly modest, the application of these goals is a difficult task indeed.

What happens now depends largely on the teachers who have formed committees to concentrate future efforts on curriculum changes, disciplinary measures, community participation, and so forth. It's up to them to work with the school boards, and up to the boards to use their power to implement change."[18]

This administrator's statement in 1968 captures many of the steps that were utilized to move from racial integration to new levels of racial understanding. Indeed, many of her suggestions laid the groundwork for the diversity, equity, and inclusion needs we are facing today. We can no longer afford "rose-colored glasses," now called "color-blindness," if we want all children to be the best that they can be.

An April 2019 article in the *Atlantic* punctuates my story. It reports how the 1960s efforts made a real difference in raising student achievement throughout the nation. "During the very brief period—roughly a decade—in which Congress and the federal courts did prioritize desegregation, the results were very encouraging. When Congress passed the 1964 Civil Rights Act, which outlawed racial discrimination, and the 1965 Elementary and Secondary Education Act, which provided federal funding to schools, the combination created an important leverage point: School districts that didn't desegregate would be barred from receiving the new influx of federal funding. The federal pressure worked, particularly in the South, where schools saw sharp reductions

---

18 "Teaching the Teachers," *Chicago Magazine*, Summer 1968.

in segregation. Black students' test scores rose, and White students' scores stayed high."[19]

Moving Forward: Creating Educational Equity Is the Challenge of This Generation

Over the last forty years, school integration became a back-burner issue at the federal level; and, with the loss of that focus, many attempts to close the achievement gap at the local or state level either failed outright or stagnated. That's why the stories we've shared with you about Illinois School Districts 202 and 98 are so important today. Those school districts achieved what few others have by creating a laser focus on inclusive cultures and providing culturally responsive curriculum—the target became educational equity.

Having been a part of the District 202 and District 98 efforts that closed the achievement gap, we can only tell you how fulfilling it was to see all—not some—but all students rise to higher achievement levels. We urge you to enjoy that same exhilaration by asking yourself:

- Where am I on my diversity, equity, and inclusion journey?
- Where do I see inequities in my educational system?
- How can I help address these inequities?

Isn't it time to "Zap the Gap"?

---

19   Richard D. Kahlenberg, Halley Potter, and Kimberly Quick, "Segregation Is Preventable. Congress Just Isn't Trying," *Atlantic*, April 18, 2019, https://www.theatlantic.com/ideas/archive/2019/04/school-integration-over-compensatory-education/587407/.

SUGGESTED READINGS FOR THOSE WHO WANT TO PURSUE EQUITY FURTHER

Alexander, Michelle. *The New Jim Crow: Mass Incarceration in the Age of Colorblindness.* New York: The New Press, 2010.

Beese, Jane A. and Jennifer L. Martin. *Teaching for Educational Equity: Case Studies for Professional Development and Principal Preparation, Vol. 2.* Lanham, MD: Rowman & Littlefield, 2017.

Brooks, Jeffrey S. *Black School, White School: Racism and Educational (Mis) Leadership.* New York: Teachers College Press, 2012.

Delpit, Lisa. *Multiplication Is for White People: Raising Expectations for Other People's Children.* New York: The New Press, 2012.

Feagin, J. R., and J. A. Cobas. *Latinos Facing Racism: Discrimination, Resistance, and Endurance.* Boulder, Colorado: Paradigm Publishers, 2014.

Gay, Geneva. *Culturally Responsive Teaching: Theory, Research, and Practice.* 3rd. ed. New York: Teachers College Press, 2018.

Hagerman, Margaret A. *White Kids: Growing Up with Privilege in a Racially Divided America.* New York: New York University Press, 2018.

Hammond, Zaretta. *Culturally responsive teaching and the brain: Promoting authentic engagement and rigor among culturally and linguistically diverse students.* Thousand Oaks, CA: Corwin Press, 2015.

Howard, Tyrone. *Why Race and Culture Matter in Schools: Closing the Achievement Gap in America's Classrooms.* New York: Teachers College Press, 2010.

Kendi, I. X., and K. Ibram X. *Stamped from the Beginning: The Definitive History of Racist Ideas in America.* New York: Nation Books, 2016.

Lindsey, Delores B., et al. *Culturally Proficient Learning Communities: Confronting Inequities Through Collaborative Curiosity.* Thousand Oaks, CA: Corwin, 2009.

O'Halloran, Susan. *www.susanohalloran.com.*

Oluo, Ijeoma. *So You Want to Talk about Race.* New York: Seal Press, 2018.

Sleeter, Christine. *Professional Development for Culturally Responsive and Relationship-Based Pedagogy: Black Studies and Critical Thinking. Volume 24.* New York: Peter Lang, 2011.

Smith, Robert and S. David Brazer. *Striving for Equity: District Leadership for Narrowing Opportunity and Achievement Gaps.* Cambridge, Massachusetts: Harvard Education Press, 2016.

Smith, R., et al. *Gaining on the Gap: Changing Hearts, Minds, and Practice.* Lanham, MD: Rowman & Littlefield Education, 2011.

Steele, Claude. *Whistling Vivaldi: And Other Clues to How Stereotypes Affect Us.* New York: W. W. Norton & Company, 2010.

Terrell, Raymond D. and Randall Lindsey. *Culturally Proficient Leadership: The Personal Journey Begins Within.* Thousand Oaks, CA: Corwin, 2009.

BRIEF BIOS OF AUTHORS AND EDITOR

Dr. Carmen I. Ayala has 36 years in education and serves as the 30th State Superintendent of Education in Illinois. She is the first woman and person of color appointed to the position. Previously, she served children and families as a bilingual and general education teacher, director, assistant superintendent, and district superintendent. She has a strong background in systemic curriculum development, which has resulted in all students being able to thrive, grow, and achieve.

Bea Young has been actively involved in supporting educational equity since her teaching days in the 1960s. She spent the summer of 1964 in Mississippi helping to develop the curriculum for the Civil Rights Freedom Schools. In 1965, she became the first education services director for the Illinois Commission on Human Relations and was later appointed to executive director. Shortly thereafter, she became a consultant in the business world where she was a pioneer in developing cultural change through diversity and inclusion for Fortune 500 companies across the country. In 2005, she returned to her first love, education, and created Bea Young Associates, LLC: Collaboration for Educational Equity.

Michael Kilgore worked as director of education and planning at the University of Chicago Hospitals and Clinics during the 1980s. Over the past four decades, he has partnered with Bea Young, managing corporate and educational change efforts related to diversity and now educational equity. He coauthored cultural audits for multiple school districts, including those for Plainfield District 202 and Berwyn North District 98. Michael is also a magazine editor, musician, and vocalist.

Susan O'Halloran is a nationally recognized professional storyteller and diversity consultant. She's been featured on PBS and ABC's *Nightline*, and in the *New York Times*. Learn about Sue's professional storytelling and diversity, equity, and inclusion seminars at *www.susanohalloran.com*. For more information about how teachers can make their curriculum more culturally relevant in the four circles of the culturally responsive curriculum model, visit Sue's online campus and her program for teachers: *Stop Walking on Eggshells: 5 Steps to Being a Racially-Skilled Teacher*.

Duane Barnes has years of experience as a retail marketing and personnel executive. He has been a member of the US Army Counter-Intelligence Corps, an adjunct professor of education, and a facilitator of diversity training. As a member of the Bea Young Associates team, he has conducted focus groups and focus group reviews. He is also a part-time basketball coach and play critic.

www.restoringthesoultoeducation.com

CPSIA information can be obtained
at www.ICGtesting.com
Printed in the USA
FSHW022313300819